More
Before

Five in a Row

Inspired learning through great books.

Ages 3-5

By Carrie Lambert Bozeman

More Before Five in a Row

First Edition

ISBN 978-1-888659-21-4

Cover design and artistic contribution by Michael Bozeman

Published by:
Five in a Row Publishing
312 SW Greenwich Dr.
Suite 220
Lee's Summit, MO 64082
816-866-8500

Send all requests for information to the above address.

To my parents: thank you for guiding me into a love of literature and learning. Mom, thank you for teaching me how to teach.

To my husband: you are my best friend and biggest encourager.

To my children: you are fearfully and wonderfully made and I am the luckiest mom—getting to spend each day with the three of you! You are teaching me the important things in life.

With special thanks to Rebekah for all her help on this project.

Contents

More Before Five in a Row

An Introduction to
More Before Five in a Row

More Before Five in a Row is a continuation of the "inspired learning through great books" which was first presented in *Before Five in a Row*. Jane Claire Lambert wrote *Before Five in a Row* and the *Five in a Row* curriculum. She also raised, taught, and inspired me. I was brought up with a love of great literature and have found great joy in teaching my children using *Before Five in a Row*, *Five in a Row*, and *Beyond Five in a Row* and passing on a love of learning through great books.

More Before Five in a Row was written to help create connections between you and your young child. It easily brings children into discussions and lessons that are interesting to them because they relate to a wonderful children's picture book. Helping our children discover that amazing stories and knowledge spring from books—not just from a handheld screen or electronic device—*is* something that we have to teach them intentionally.

In the following pages, you'll find quick, connection-building lessons for you and your child to enjoy together. There are many learning activities that are guided through play; an *essential* component for a young child to retain information that they've discovered. Most of the lessons are discussion-based. Oral learning is important because young children can process and wonder about things far beyond their ability to read or write. Children are learning all the time by asking questions and listening to your answers. It is a *natural* learning method and helps them maintain a *desire* to learn; one that might be stifled by the struggle of producing physical work.

Studies have shown not only that reading to your child is important, but that *how* you read to them is also of great significance. Asking your child questions as you read, having your child put themselves in a character's place, and discussing feelings all deepen your child's understanding of the story and help build intellectual empathy, which can then be put into practice in their own lives.

The *More Before Five in a Row* lessons use this strategy (it's all provided for you: the questions, what to point out, etc.) to help deepen your child's connections to the stories, to others, and to the world around them!

The Six Early Literacy Skills

We all want to give our children the foundation and building blocks necessary to do well in their education. *More Before Five in a Row* builds many lessons around six early literacy skills. These six skills initially appeared in the first edition of *Every Child Ready to Read* and were based on the research of Dr. C. J. Lonigan and Dr. G. C. Whitehurst. The order in which you teach them does not matter; they are skills that interact with each other and that your child can learn in any order.

You can introduce these skills to your child during specific learning times or throughout your daily rhythms. They are referenced and explained in the manual lessons so that you can take these skills and apply them to any activity the two of you enjoy together.

The six early literacy skills are:

1. Vocabulary
Reading to your child and allowing them to hear words is one of the best ways your child can build their early vocabulary. Developing a personal love of reading will help your child discover new vocabulary words regardless of their learning level or life stage.

2. Narrative Skills
These skills include storytelling, sequencing events, being able to describe things, and guessing what might happen. A child's ability to use these skills effectively shows that they are comprehending what they are reading. This skill can be developed by asking your child questions about what you read to them.

3. Print Awareness
Knowing how a book works—right side up, left to right, etc., is a print awareness skill. Notice with your child where print appears: road signs, newspapers, books, signage, cereal boxes, etc. What are the symbols that appear at the end of the sentence? A period, question mark, and exclamation point; what do they look like, and why do we use them? These are all part of print awareness.

4. Phonological Awareness
Phonological awareness is being aware of what sounds are in a word. Breaking words into smaller pieces and hearing those separate sounds will help your child when they are learning to read. Rhyming, singing songs, or choosing a letter sound to listen for (when reading together or playing an alphabet game) will help your child develop their phonological awareness.

5. Letter Knowledge
Letter knowledge includes:

- realizing that letters are different from each other
- seeing alphabet letters everywhere
- knowing each letter's sound
- knowing the letter's name

Before a child can read, they have to understand that groups of letters make up a word.

6. Print Motivation

Getting your child interested in and enjoying books is great motivation to learn how to read for themselves—that's what print motivation is all about. Find books your *child* likes and have fun reading together! Stop or change your approach if they lose interest. For a young child you might read a book in several shorter sections with a related activity or playtime in between. You could even start a book in the morning and finish it together at bedtime. Let your child color or play with blocks, playdough, or Kinetic Sand™ while you read to keep their attention during a longer story.

An Encouragement for *You*

I wrote *More Before Five in a Row* as a preschool curriculum, but also specifically to be an encouragement to *you*. While writing this manual I was homeschooling an older child but also parenting and teaching a 2-year-old and 4-year-old. Having small children is amazing, exhausting, messy, and beautiful. I know some days you're too busy to find time for a shower or get more than one swallow of hot coffee. (I've learned to love cold coffee!) Sometimes I found that my quiet time or devotional consisted only of the storybook Bible that I read to my children before bed. Storybook Bibles are good, but I needed a bit more for my own spiritual nourishment.

One way I hope *More Before* encourages you is through the separate Bible lesson written for *you*, the parent! It is not for you to read to your child, but to read for yourself! Then as you read the *More Before* story selection (probably dozens of times if your children are anything like mine) perhaps you'll find a moment to remember the thoughts shared, pause, take a deep breath, and be refreshed.

Sincerely,
Carrie Lambert Bozeman

4

Making the Most of
More Before Five in a Row

With grateful appreciation to Jane Claire Lambert,
*author of **Before Five in a Row** and the original*
version of this "Making the Most of" section.

What delights a young child? There are many things, but for most children having someone read them a book is near the top of the list. To luxuriate in the security of a person who will give a child their time, allowing the child to snuggle as close as they want, and share with them a wonderful story is one of the highlights of childhood! Sometimes a child wants the same story read over and over again. Because the stories are simple ones, this repetition may become tiring for the reader. So *More Before Five in a Row* suggests a wide variety of interesting topics and activities to present, now and then, after a story is read. These discussions and activities provide added interest for both the reader and the child.

The stories included are wonderful stories for early childhood. Because they are *good* stories, you, along with your older children, will likely find yourselves appreciating them. But this series of "little lessons" was created especially to bring enjoyment to children ages three through five. The point is not so much to *instruct* or *teach* as it is to have a happy introduction to books, provide an interesting, light introduction to many different topics, and to build intimacy between the reader and child. The topical subject headings are only to *suggest* in what areas these activities might *lay a foundation* for academic subjects to be encountered by your child in later grades.

More Before Five in a Row lessons are written for ages three through five. This manual is a bridge between the early preschool lessons of *Before Five in a Row* and the more academic ones found in *Five in a Row*. The lessons found in this manual are designed to introduce your child to the different academic subjects found within *Five in a Row* while maintaining the playful learning style of *Before*.

Remember that three-year-olds cover a vast range of differing abilities. Some three-year-olds will not yet be able to sit still through an entire story, let alone answer questions or discuss it. They may not want to hunt for items in the illustrations. That's perfectly normal. There are many other ideas in the lessons that revolve around play that you can make use of now and save the lessons which require more focus for six months or a year. If you are patient, there will come a day when your child delights in the "story activities," and in the meantime you will have had lots of fun playing together.

Many of the stories used in *More Before* are simple. Some have less detail than other picture books in terms of setting or illustration. Yet each of them has a special warmth and charm that keeps your child wanting to experience them over and over. Several of the stories included have repetitious wording. A young child finds it challenging to be able to tell a story before it's finished. Repetition helps them learn and remember the story so they know it well enough to beat you to the punch line. In addition, rereading the story several times allows you to make different comments at each reading. Keep your teaching subtle and your child will enjoy both the stories and the related activities you share together.

For each story title chosen for *More Before Five in a Row* you will find suggested activities. These activities can follow the reading of the stories. Many times you will read a story and not do *any* activity directly following it. Other times you will decide to bring up a topic and talk it over together. You might choose to read one of the stories during the day and save a question or discussion for lunch or dinner time. You could say, "Remember when we read about the little bear and his little boat? What problem did he have? How did he solve his problem?" You can even bring up activities or questions from previously read stories when you are on a walk together, standing in line at the supermarket, or during bath time, etc. *Anytime* is a good time to share the stories and activities that build a warm closeness between a parent and child.

You will undoubtedly read many other stories not included in *More Before Five in a Row*. There are wonderful Richard Scarry stories, the beloved books of Dr. Seuss, Beatrix Potter, and many, many more waiting to be discovered and read. But, when you want a special story with "ready to use" activities and ideas that inspire creative interaction, pick up a *More Before* story and enjoy!

The subject heading listed at each story activity shows how the ideas in *More Before Five in a Row* lay the foundations for *future* formal academic training in each of these subject areas. *More Before* is *not* attempting to teach academics, but rather to provide a strong foundation of academic "readiness." Resist the temptation to try to create three-year-old professors. In the long run, pushing preschoolers to leap tall academic buildings in a single bound does *not* produce the results most parents want. Metaphorically speaking, it's like trying to teach a child to walk before they've mastered scooting, rolling, and crawling! Some children might be able to learn academic material at a very early age, but vital maturity steps have been skipped in the rush.

Above all, the time between ages three and five should be a time of sharing, hugging, reading, singing, dancing, puzzles, blocks, outdoor excursions, swinging high, playing in the sandbox, and enjoying fascinating introductions to the wonderful world of life.

The ideas presented in *More Before Five in a Row* are not meant to teach in depth, but only to enhance your child's awareness of the world around them and create memorable times of interaction between you. So, don't take the academic subject headings too seriously. They are only provided to show *you* what areas of future learning you'll be developing.

You'll also find an Animal Classification Game, a Storybook Map, and Story Disks at the end of the manual for additional hands-on fun and as a transition to some of the memorable teaching elements found in *Five in a Row*. Finally, a Bible verse and devotional (one for you and another for your child) has been included for each lesson plan, if you care to use it.

Besides the *More Before Five in a Row* stories and activities, make sure that you participate in many different kinds of play with your child. Take time to enjoy the wonders of nature together. Whether gazing at the stars or watching an industrious ant or bee, it is good to appreciate God's creation. Spend lots of time together searching for exciting examples of beauty and wonder.

Remember too, that activities in which you take the time to include your child, such as going to a children's play, short music or dance programs, or even trips to certain interesting stores all help to broaden their experience of life. They becomes more aware and pleasantly excited about the world around them, stimulating their natural curiosity and desire to know more.

This *desire* to learn is the foundation you want firmly in place *long before* you begin their formal academic training. When a child is excited and curious, they *want* to learn!

When you have little children you may hear, "The days are long, but the years are short." As a mother to two young children, I'm well aware of how long the days can seem. But, as a mother to an older child as well, I am beginning to see the truth in the second part of this saying. Savor these moments with your little ones. Build connections, get to know *them*, and enjoy creating memories that will last a lifetime!

"The days are long, but the years are short."

Savor these moments with your little ones. Build connections, get to know *them*, and enjoy creating memories that will last a lifetime!

ALL THE WORLD

10

Title: *All the World*
Author: Liz Garton Scanlon
Illustrator: Marla Frazee
Copyright: 2009

Summary

A poetic connection between all the things that make up the world around us and how we fit into the world.

Bible

For Parent:

The next-to-last page of the story reads, "Hope and peace and love and trust," followed by the final page's words, "All the world is all of us."

This story selection is a beautiful example of people coming together, along with family and community, to help each other and love one another. Seeing the positive in humanity and knowing that we are capable of being a hope-filled, peaceful, loving, and trusting group is something to strive for, encourage, and teach our children.

But sometimes, this is not the side of people that we see, or even that we are to others. More than we'd like to admit, we fail at these endeavors when our human nature kicks in. Romans 15:13 is encouraging, though, showing us how with God's help, when we trust in him, we can succeed in being a person full of hope, peace, and love.

Romans 15:13, "May the God of hope fill you with all joy and **peace** as you **trust** in him, so that you may overflow with **hope** by the power of the Holy Spirit."

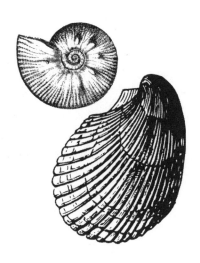

"Overflowing with hope" is something that we could all use more of in our lives. As you read this book with your child, remember that "Hope and peace and love and trust," can be something you share with those around you; something that effortlessly spills over from the excess that God has poured into you.

Read our verse, once again, as a personal blessing ... Romans 15:13, "May the God of hope fill *you* with all joy and **peace** as you **trust** in him, so that you may overflow with **hope** by the power of the Holy Spirit."

For Child:

Our story talks about people in the world: us, others, parts of the whole, *All the World*. John 3:16a "For God so loved the world..." is a perfect verse to begin teaching a young child about God's love for each of us. This is just a portion of John 3:16, because shortened verses provide an opportunity for even young children to learn and remember God's words.

God created the world and everything and everyone in it. All of the things that are mentioned in our story were created by God. All the people shown in the story are loved by God.

As you read the story with your child for the second or third time, you can say, "Rock, stone, pebble, sand," God created those things. "Body, shoulder, arm, hand," God made our bodies. "Nanas, papas, cousins, kin," God loves each of them!

In full, John 3:16 says, "For God so loved the world that he gave his one and only Son, that whoever believes in him shall not perish but have eternal life." As your child gets older, they can learn the entire verse and what God did to provide eternal life for those that believe in him. For now, they can learn why ... because God loved **all the world**!

Language Arts: Whole to Part

Young children are learning and making connections throughout their day. They learn through hands-on activities and experiences, visual content that they are taking in through their eyes, and auditory content through what they hear. Reading to your child is a beautiful way to encourage their language development.

All the World uses a series of words to relate a whole to its parts throughout the story. "Body, shoulder, arm, hand," is one example where you have a whole (body) followed by some of its parts (shoulder, arm, hand). Another example, "Tree, trunk, branch, crown," starts with the whole (tree) and then its parts, (trunk, branch, crown).

This is an excellent way to help a young child build their vocabulary and make those connections between words. They might know the word "hand," but not yet know shoulder or arm. Or they might know rock, but after reading the story, they learn of an interrelationship between rock, stone, pebble, and sand. Hearing those words connected forms an association between them.

You can make this into a game with your child to play in the car, in a waiting room, or anytime, just for fun. You say a word and have your child think of a word that is associated with your word. For example, you could say, "butterfly" and your child could say, "wings or flutter or caterpillar." Have your child start with a word, and you name something related to their word. To make it harder, list two or three associated items, the way our story does.

Art: Whole-to-Part Collage

To reinforce the Language Arts lesson or as an alternate lesson, help your child find pictures in a magazine (or go online and print some) of related words and make a collage. Search for images of words from the story or make up your own. Examples: table, bowl, cup, spoon; or nest, bird, feather, fly.

Glue the images onto white paper. Layer them and draw on or around them. Any artistic expression works for this project!

Science: Rock, Stone, Pebble, Sand - Weathering and Erosion

Rocks are formed when mountains or boulders break into smaller pieces. Stones are made as those rocks split, then pebbles are created as the stones separate, and lastly, sand is produced as the pebbles disintegrate.

Weathering is a factor that can cause rocks to break. Water and freezing water/ice, contribute to expansion and contraction in the rock that causes breakage. Waves, wind, currents, rivers, and glaciers can all move weathered rock from one place to another through erosion. This also contributes to further breakdown. As you read the story to your child, you can explain how a rock can become a stone, a pebble, or sand through weathering and erosion.

Go for a nature walk in search of rocks, stones, pebbles, or sand. See if you can find examples of some or all, and bring home samples or take pictures (print them out) to glue onto a paper and label. Help your child begin thinking like a scientist, by teaching them how to collect specimens and label them.

Playing in a sandbox or plastic bin filled with sand is always a favorite childhood activity. Kinetic Sand™ can be a less messy experience for indoor play. It is also more moldable (without needing water) and can be used to build a sandcastle. You can purchase Kinetic Sand™ or look online for instructions on making your own.

12

Science: Body, Shoulder, Arm, Hand - Body Parts

For young children, learning through songs and games is a great way to broaden their knowledge and vocabulary of body parts.

"Head, Shoulders, Knees and Toes" is a fun nursery rhyme song with hand motions that helps children learn many body parts. Here are the lyrics and hand motions. (Search Head, Shoulders, Knees and Toes online to hear or learn the tune to which it is sung.)

Head, shoulders, knees and toes,
Knees and toes.

Head, shoulders, knees and toes,
Knees and toes.

And eyes, and ears, and mouth,
And nose.

Head, shoulders, knees and toes,
Knees and toes.

Place both hands on parts of the body as they are mentioned. On the second time speed up, and get faster with each verse.

Where's your _____? is another game you can play with children. Simply fill in the blank with a body part of choice and have them touch that part of their body to answer. You'll say, "Where's your chin?" and your child will touch their chin. If they don't know, you touch their chin and say, "Here's your chin." This is a fun game to use as a distraction when you need to get clothes or a diaper on a squirming child.

Science: Seashells

A shell is a hard, protective outer layer that a sea or freshwater animal creates as part of its body. The shells you find washed up on a beach are empty because the animal has died and the softer parts have been eaten by other sea animals.

Shells, or seashells, are beautiful and vary in shape, color, and texture. If you live near a beach, you can go for a nature walk and gather shells with your child. If you can't visit a beach, take this opportunity to look for books from the library on seashells. You can also buy bags of shells at craft stores to sort (by shape, size, color), count, or glue onto collages.

Geography: Bodies of Water - Oceans, Lakes, and Streams

As you read this story with your child, you'll notice that it begins on a beach. Throughout the story, we see the beach and the sea. Near the end of the story on the moonlit page, we also clearly see a small **lake** with a **stream** leading down to the **ocean**.

After reading the first few pages and seeing the children playing in the sand at the beach, you turn the page and see the ocean with waves pushing up towards the shore and a road on the land up above the sea. You can talk with your child and point out how the ocean is vast, and the water comes right up to the land.

Oceans have waves that are caused by the gravitational pull of the sun and moon on the earth. This is called tides or tidal waves. You can help your child experiment with creating waves in the bathtub or an outdoor water table or bin filled with water. Pushing or pulling the water with our hands makes the water move one way or another, the same way that gravity pulls or pushes the water in an ocean to make waves.

On the moonlit page, you can show your child how, unlike the ocean, a lake is smaller and surrounded by land. A small lake doesn't have large waves like an ocean.

Another difference you can discuss with your child is that lakes are full of fresh water, whereas oceans are full of salt water. You can get two glasses and put plain water in one and mix a small amount of salt into the second glass. Have your child taste the difference between fresh water and salt water.

Science: Gardens, Bees, and Pollination

We see neighbors gathered in a garden, picking vegetables and beekeeping. Did your child notice the two figures in the "funny" white outfits with hats that have veils over their faces?

Tell your child that the people are harvesting honey from the beehive and explain that they wear the white outfits with gloves and veils to keep the bees from landing on them. Bees are good to have near a garden since they do the work of pollinating the crops, which ensures seed production and future plants.

Notice the flowers outside the garden fence. Flowers are often planted near vegetable gardens to draw bees to the garden. Bees are attracted to the colorful and rewarding flowers and will pollinate nearby vegetables once they've been drawn to the area.

Here's a interesting activity that can teach children how a bee takes pollen from one flower to another. Fill a bowl (this bowl represents one flower) with cheese curls and have your child move them around for a while or snack on them. Meanwhile, draw a quick outline of a flower onto a white piece of paper. Now have your child rub or wipe their fingers on the white paper flower. The orange bits of "pollen" from the cheese curls are transferred to the flower. (See the Science: Insects - Bees lesson in the *Go to Sleep Little Farm* unit for more information on bees.)

In the same way, pollen sticks to bees' legs which is then carried with them to another flower where it rubs off. This transfer of pollen grains from the male anther of a flower to the female stigma is what allows for possible reproduction of the flower.

Social Studies: Farmer's Markets

"All the world's a garden bed." Looking at the illustration on this page, we see a place where the community is coming together to buy and sell fruits, vegetables, and flowers. This is a farmer's market. Ask your child if they would enjoy shopping outside in the fresh air, instead of inside a grocery store. This is an excellent opportunity to visit a farmer's market if you have one near you.

Farmer's markets allow farmers to bring fresh produce straight from their garden to the local community. The product is as newly harvested as possible, and by avoiding shipping it to a store, the cost can be lower for the customer. Often you can buy flowers, baked goods, soaps, or other handmade items at a farmer's market. It's a beautiful opportunity to join friends and neighbors from your community and support local farmers and artisans.

Imaginary play is a great way for children to learn more about the world and everything in it. (If you're able to visit a farmer's market, your child will have more reference for this game; if you aren't able to, this will provide your little one a chance to imagine doing so, and you can help direct them on what to do.) Gather real or pretend fruits, vegetables, and flowers, along with other small items in your home (candles, jam or jelly, homemade cookies). Use real or pretend money and take turns pretending to be the "farmer" selling the items and the customer buying the items.

Science: Parts of a Tree

On the page with the illustration of the children climbing the giant tree, point out the parts of a tree that were listed on the previous page of the story. The trunk, branch, and crown are all parts of the whole tree.

The trunk is the large part of the tree coming out of the ground up to the point that branches start coming off of the trunk. Branches are the parts of the tree that stretch out as wide as possible to hold many, many leaves. The leaves make up the crown of the tree and catch the sunlight, which helps the tree produce the fuel it needs to grow. The branches and leaves also collect and direct rainwater to the base of the tree. The leaves block sunlight on the ground below the tree, which helps keep other competing plants from growing. Roots, while underground and unseen, are essential to the tree. They store nutrients for the tree during cold winter months and transport water and minerals from the ground up to the other systems in the tree.

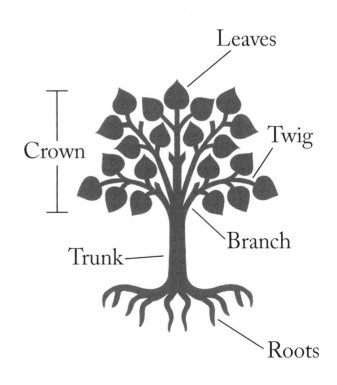

Health: Climbing Trees - Appropriate Risk-Taking for Developmental Growth

The children in our story enjoy climbing an enormous old tree. They climb up and sit on the branches, legs dangling. While your child might still be too young to climb trees, it's good to begin thinking about how and why children benefit from active play and challenging activities.

While wanting to keep our children safe and free from injury is a worthy goal, it can sometimes hinder our willingness to allow our children to take risks. Taking risks is something that children want and need for their development. It enables them to explore their limits and have new experiences. Through managed risk-taking opportunities, they will develop coordination, learn how to take appropriate risks, experience natural consequences, and learn to negotiate their environment, along with other vital skills.

"Be careful!" How many times do we say or yell this to our children? But young children often don't know how to "be careful." Changing what we say can help teach our child the skills they need to be safer.

Instead of saying "be careful," try helping your child become aware of their surroundings by saying things like, "**Do you see** ... that wet rock, the muddy bank, your friend standing right there?" Or, "**Try moving** ... that hand up higher, the rock out of your way." "**Could you** ... run faster, put your arms out for better balance?" This type of communication shows your child what to look for or how to use their body to take risks more safely.

Help your child manage their own risk by learning to problem solve. Asking them questions like, "**What's your plan** ... to cross that creek, climb up to that branch?" Other queries such as, "**Who can help you ..., What can you use to..., What else can you try...?**" will all help your child think through their actions and assess the consequences before taking the risk.

While injuries are upsetting to parent and child alike, minor injuries are a part of normal childhood development. To encourage parents in this stretching endeavor, here are some of the benefits of taking appro-

16

priate risks: higher self-confidence, enjoyment of new activities, gaining self-awareness, and becoming emotionally and physically stronger!

Social Studies: Transportation

Ask your child to notice in the story all the different ways that people are getting from one place to another. You can make a list together as you read through the story.

We see people driving cars, scooters, and tractors; walking, running, climbing, and boating; and riding tricycles and bicycles. There's a baby in a backpack carrier and a baby being pushed in a stroller. We can see a surfboard in the back of a truck. A dog is riding in a wagon.

See how many of these your child can point out to you as you read through the story. The next time you read it, they'll likely point out even more ways people are moving from place to place.

Set up a small town scene with toy cars, plastic figures, doll houses, blocks, or anything else you have on hand. You can act out going to the beach, climbing a tree, eating at a cafe, or any other favorite scenes from the story.

Character Development: Nurturing Resilience

Resilience is the ability to recover quickly from difficulties. It's such an essential skill for children to learn. All too often, we jump in and comfort a child who's facing a challenge, or we fix their problem for them. Parents react this way out of love and as a result of the discomfort that they feel when watching their child go through something hurtful, scary, or hard. This response can cause its own issues, though. A child who's been rescued, without a chance to solve their own problem, doesn't learn resilience. They might think they aren't strong enough or capable of solving their own problems.

If we, as parents, can learn to sit with that uncomfortable feeling for just a few seconds (or minutes) longer than we want to, our children will have a chance to work out the issue on their own. Through that opportunity, they will gain confidence in themselves that is worth far more than the momentary discomfort the parent might feel.

If there is something a child can do, let them, and encourage them! Nurture that feeling of *ability* and being able to try hard things, whether they succeed or end up needing help. Resilience isn't just about doing everything on their own. Remind them that being brave and strong also means knowing when to ask for help. Asking for help can be a tough and brave thing to do. Not succeeding isn't a failure; it's merely your first attempt at success.

In our story, a challenging situation occurs when the rain comes and disrupts the fun day at the lake. "Slip, trip, stumble, fall ... All the world goes round this way." Reading stories that aren't all sunshine and success will help build emotional reserves for moments in their own lives that don't go as planned.

Reframing a situation and looking for the positive is another tool to help nurture your child's resilience. So instead of saying, "Oh man, this rain is horrible, and now we can't play at the beach anymore," you might exclaim, "Wow, I didn't expect it to rain today. What can we do in the rain that we wouldn't be able to if it were sunny?" Focus on what you *can* do, rather than what you *can't* do.

Health: Calming Down - End of Day

Following an eventful day in the community, the sun begins to set, shadows lengthen, and we begin to see lovely examples of how to calm and settle comfortably into the evening. A man and woman are reading and knitting quietly together as the sun sets outside their window. Children are warming themselves near the fire in the dim light. Someone is walking on a pier as the last bit of sun dips below the ocean. We see family and friends gathered together enjoying music by the warm lamplight.

One way to encourage calm and help ready your child for sleep is to designate a time each evening to turn off all screens and just be with one another. Reading, playing a calming game, talking, watching the sunset, stargazing, listening to music, or any activity that your family enjoys can provide time and space for a child to relax and release the day's tensions. Allowing extra time to talk before bed can be beneficial if you have an anxious child or one who just loves to talk.

Ask your child to look for all the different ways that the characters in the story calm down and connect as the day comes to a close. Have them pick their favorites and if it's something that you don't already do together, try it out.

Social Studies: How We Fit into the World

Throughout the story, we've been looking at the world and many of the things in it. Nearing the end of the book, the focus shifts from all things in the world, to us and how we are a part of the world.

We as people, along with every other person in the world, together make up humanity. "All the world is you and me." We are in this life and the world together. Every person holds value and a place in our society that is important, and that no one else can fill.

Begin to help your child find the similarities and connections they have with the people they meet. This is especially important to facilitate when people are different from your child. When your child meets someone with different abilities, hair color, skin tone, religion, opinions, age, size, language, social status, or any other difference, encourage them to see

18

the things that make them similar to that person. You might say to your child, "Isn't it neat how that little girl treats her brother nicely, just like you?" Or, "That man might not be able to walk very fast anymore, but I bet he was as fast as you when he was your age." Maybe you'd say, "Yes, she looks different and can't speak, but did you see how much she loved to swim? She loves swimming as much as you do!"

Finding our commonality helps us to push past initial shyness or unease caused by our differences and get to know someone better. That knowledge is what allows us to love and trust people, which in turn allows for more hope and peace in our world.

All the World is a story of our shared connections. Each of us on earth shares in what our world provides us: trees, shells, gardens, oceans, sunsets, etc. We also share a human bond, with everyone else on earth, that allows us to provide things for one another, like food, comfort, warmth, and relationships, as well as "hope and peace and love and trust."

*Have your child place the story disk for **All the World** on the storybook map at the farmer's market.*

Title: *Baby Bear Sees Blue*

Author: Ashley Wolff

Illustrator: Ashley Wolff

Copyright: 2012

20

Summary

Baby Bear wakes in the den with Mama Bear and starts a day of discovery and learning about the colors and things that make up the world around him. A sweet introduction to colors and nature!

Bible

For Parent:

Deuteronomy 6:6-7, "These commandments that I give you today are to be on your hearts. Impress them on your children. Talk about them when you sit at home and when you walk along the road, when you lie down and when you get up."

Just like Mama Bear, you have an opportunity to teach your children God's word, his commandments, and about the fantastic world around them that God created! Be encouraged today that you are doing important work … messy, exhausting, fun, beautiful work.

For Child:

Genesis 9:13a," I have set my rainbow in the clouds…"
God put the rainbow in the sky after the rain! God created the rainbow, and all of its beautiful colors.

Language Arts: Book Title

Your child might notice after reading the story together a few times, that there is a page in the book that repeats the book title. When Baby Bear hears the birds singing, and Mama Bear tells him it's the jays, on the next page it says, "Baby Bear sees blue." If your child doesn't catch this after several readings, you can point it out by saying, "Hey, did you notice, these are the same words as the name of the book?" The author/illustrator might have chosen this part of the book to highlight as the title because of the lovely alliteration.

Language Arts: Alliteration

The title uses alliteration (repetition of two or more consonant sounds at the beginning of nearby words; in this case, the letter B) **B**aby **B**ear Sees **B**lue. This is a literary device that is common in children's nursery rhymes and in content aimed at children because it is memorable and sometimes funny-sounding, and can help call the reader's attention to a sentence. Bob the Builder, Mickey Mouse, and "Peter Piper Picked a Peck of Pickled Peppers" are just a few examples of alliteration.

Have fun with your child by putting together words that start with the same letter. **P**ick **p**up up. **D**og's **d**ay is **d**one. **J**ust **j**ump up and **j**itter. If they join in —excellent! Or if they just giggle while you say silly sentences, that's perfect too!

Alliteration builds phonological awareness, an early literacy skill, through hearing and playing with the sounds of words. (This is one of six early literacy skills; see the introduction to *More Before* for the entire list.)

Here's a list of a few alliterative books for young children to continue the fun!

Dr. Seuss's ABC: An Amazing Alphabet Book! by Dr. Seuss
Sheep in a Jeep by Nancy E. Shaw
Jamberry by Bruce Degen

Art: Color

The story is full of exciting introductions to many different colors! Yellow, green, blue, brown, red, orange, gray, and black. The author ties each color to an item in nature, which creates a lovely and intuitive learning experience.

Coloring or painting with your child is a fun way to play with and begin learning the colors they are hearing in the book. After reading through a time or two, have them color a picture as you read the story. Your child might use each color as you mention them or they might not. It doesn't matter if they color something from the story or not; just allowing them to listen while coloring can be an excellent experience for them!

Teaching Tip:
Young children are often restless and don't sit for an entire book, but allowing them to move around, color, use playdough, or build with wood blocks or LEGO® bricks while listening might allow for a pleasant extended reading time together. There are different learning styles as well, and auditory learners will often remember and learn just as well or better by listening without looking at the book. This style of teaching/learning can grow with your child and extend into their grade school days.

Art: Drama

After reading the story together, act out certain scenes with your child. The opening page offers an opportunity to yawn, blink, and stretch! Enjoy the giggles as you act out the story and see if your child can mimic your actions or do them on his own. You can wave, sing, wade, sniff, give butterfly kisses (fluttering your eyelash on your child's cheek), growl, and peek ... these are fun to do as you read the corresponding page of the story or even as a Simon Says-type game, throughout your day.

Science: The Five Senses

The five senses (touch, sight, hearing, smell, and taste) are introduced to your child through the sweet story of Baby Bear's day. Baby Bear **feels** the sun warming his body, the fish splashing water onto him, and the butterfly tickling him. He **sees** the leaves dancing, the trout, the rainbow, and all the colors and animals around him in the story. Birds call out, and Baby Bear **hears** them singing. He also **hears** the thunder rumble. The scent of strawberries on the breeze in the meadow allows Baby Bear to **smell** and find them. After smelling the delicious strawberries, Baby Bear **tastes** them!

Ask your child what they feel, see, hear, smell, and taste throughout the day as the opportunity arises. You can also set up interesting **sensory experiences** for them to enter into.

A sensory experience to go along with this story might include some leaves on a twig to tickle each other (feel). A bird song to listen to (hear) outside, or look up "bird song mp3" on the computer to listen to a specific bird (like the jays in the story). Strawberries cut up and ready to snack on (taste) ... don't forget to smell them first! Make sure to point out what your child is seeing (sight) throughout the experience.

You can provide your child with all sorts of sensory play daily, almost effortlessly, and without having to plan or buy things. Here are some ideas to get you started:

- Smelling herbs together is a fun and simple way to talk about your sense of smell.

- Tasting opportunities are naturally placed throughout your day with meals and snacks, and can be discussed to help your child think about what they're tasting (sour, salty, sweet, bitter).

- Listen for exciting or new sounds to point out to your child: sirens, trains, car horns, crickets, the sound of the wind blowing through the trees, birds, etc. Talk about what they can hear and what sounds they like or dislike.

- We see things all day long! "I spy with my little eye…" is a fun game for young children and can help them focus on using their sense of sight to notice things around them.

- Our sense of touch is the first sense we develop! Before a baby can smell, taste, hear, or see, they can feel things. This helps babies with safety, security, and learning. Babies feel objects to learn about them. Scientists have even found that touch can support language development. Pointing to words in books as you say the word can help your child recognize words faster. Encourage your child to touch and explore the world around them! (The five senses are covered again in science lessons for *In a Blue Room*.)

Teaching Tip:
Games are a great way to teach children new skills!

Science: Trees - Oak

Looking at trees on walks can be a lovely way to notice the differences between trees. Different kinds of trees have differently shaped leaves, bark, and branches. Making leaf rubbings (lay a leaf under a piece of paper and roll over it evenly with an unwrapped crayon) is an interesting way to see the shape of each leaf

and make a fun memory together.

You might find acorns while on a nature walk with you child. Acorns are the fruit of the oak tree. Often you can find a cluster of acorns attached to a twig with oak leaves on it; this is a natural way for your child to see/learn that they are both from the same tree.

Science: Birds - Jays

The jays that are in *Baby Bear Sees Blue* are called Steller's jays. They are common in western United States mountain regions and forests which is where Baby Bear likely lives. If you live east of the Rocky Mountains, you might be more familiar with the

Blue jay   *Stellar's jay*

blue jay. If you're playing the Animal Classification Game, create your own card by drawing or cutting out a picture and gluing it to an index card. Or use the Stellar's jay card provided in the index to add to your collection.

Looking for birds with your child through the window (you'll have even better viewing if you have a bird feeder or make one) or on walks is a great way to notice their different colorings, shapes, sizes, and songs!

If your child shows interest in birds, use your library to find more books about birds, feathers, and nests. Here are a few to get you started:

Baby's First Book of Birds & Colors by Phyllis Limbacher Tildes

Birds Board Book by Kevin Henkes

Mrs. Peanuckle's Bird Alphabet by Mrs. Peanuckle

You Nest Here With Me by Jane Yolen; Heidi E.Y. Stemple

Craft Idea:
Help your child make a natural bird feeder to hang in a nearby tree and watch the birds enjoy their treat. Find a pinecone or use an empty toilet paper roll, coat it in peanut butter, and then roll it in bird seed. You can tie a string to the pinecone or through the empty roll and then tie the other end onto a tree branch.

24

Science: Fish - Trout

After being splashed by a fish while wading in the river, Baby Bear peers into the stream and sees a brown trout. Fish are fascinating creatures to talk about with your child.

Where do they live? In water, oceans, lakes, streams, rivers, creeks, and ponds.

How do they breathe? Fish have gills that take oxygen out of the water around them.

Going to look at fish at an aquarium or pet store is fun and makes for a great learning field trip together (also look for a Bass Pro or other large

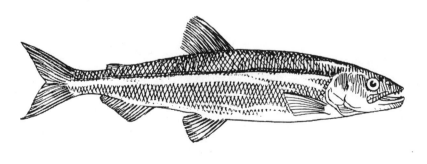

store that might have an aquarium to view fish). If you're playing the Animal Classification Game, create your own card by drawing or cutting out a picture and gluing it to an index card. Or use the trout card provided in the index to add to your collection.

A couple fun go-along books to continue investigating fish are:

A Good Day's Fishing by James Prosek

H is for Hook: A Fishing Alphabet by Judy Young

Teaching Tip:
ABC books with specific themes, like the fishing alphabet book above, are a fantastic way to build your child's vocabulary. They contain many words that relate to a specific theme. It could be the ABC's of cooking, fishing, boating, or flowers. Reading many different alphabet books will give your child new sets of vocabulary words relating to many different subjects/topics.

Safety: Weather - Thunderstorms

After reading the story with your child a time or two, see if they notice what Mother Bear does when the thunder rumbles. Your conversation might go something like this:

"Hey, what does Mother Bear do when Baby Bear asks, 'Who is growling at me?'"

Your child might say, "She says, let's hurry home."

"Yes, that's right! Why do you think she wants them to hurry home?"

"To stay dry or to be safe."

"Yes, she knows they'll be safe inside their home, and they can come out after the storm passes by. We go inside when it storms too. It's nice to stay dry and watch the rain and hear the thunder while being inside our cozy home!"

Discussions like these are great introductions for young children about safety in different situations. Learning about ways to be safe through a good story makes it easy for them to remember and also feel less frightened when they face a storm in real life.

Science: Rainbow

After the thunderstorm passes by, Baby Bear looks out and sees a rainbow! The colors of the rainbow are red, orange, yellow, green, blue, indigo, and violet. Here are some interesting rainbow facts you can share with an older child: You can only see a rainbow when it is sunny and raining at the same time. When looking at a rainbow from the ground, you see the arch or bow (half circle), but if you were able to view a rainbow from the air (on an airplane), it would be a complete circle.

Health: Rest

Share with your child how rest is an essential part of each day for all of us! Notice how Mama and Baby Bear curl up together at the end of their long day. After playing all day, our bodies need to sleep so that we can be ready to play again tomorrow. Rest helps our brains work so that we can remember things. It helps our bodies heal and keeps us healthy, so we don't get sick as often.

Discussing what you can do to make it easier to go to sleep at night is a great thing to do with young children. You can ask them questions like: What helps you to feel calm and happy? Do you like warm blankets or a light sheet? Do you want to read a story together or listen to a quiet song? Which pajamas would you like tonight? Using a few of these questions as part of a bed-time routine can be helpful. It gives the child a sense of power or choice in what's happening.

Starting a calm-down routine can be an excellent way to allow kids' brains and bodies to slow down and be ready to go to sleep when they head to bed. Here are a few ways to help calm a child before bedtime:

- A warm bath is often a terrific calming tool for babies and children.

- Turn screens off at least 30 minutes before bedtime. The blue light coming from TVs, iPads, etc., keeps the brain active and makes it hard to calm down and sleep.

- Slow rocking or rhythmic patting can help calm a tired child.

- Does your child enjoy being tightly wrapped up with a blanket, like a hot dog or burrito, while you read a story or sing a song before bed? This can calm a child in a similar way to a big hug. It's the same concept as swaddling a baby, and can be a useful technique for overactive kids who have a hard time calming down. (Note: Some children do not enjoy the feeling of being tightly wrapped, so be sensitive to what is comfortable for your child!)

- Fidget toys, a squishy ball, or a well-loved stuffed animal can be played with or held during story time. The tactile input is calming to many children and can help them quietly pay attention.

- A lightly warmed heat pack can be a lovely thing for your child to snuggle up to, especially during winter (just warm, not too hot!) Some heat packs or hot water bottles are even made in the form of stuffed animals. You can add a drop of lavender, vanilla or another favorite essential oil to the heat pack to add another calming sensory experience.

*The story disk for **Baby Bear Sees Blue** can be placed on the storybook map at the cave/den location.*

26

BLUE ON BLUE

Title: *Blue on Blue*
Author: Dianne White
Illustrator: Beth Krommes
Copyright: 2014

Summary

It's a beautiful blue and white day until a storm comes. Lots of lightning, thunder, raining, raining, raining, and then—it stops. A day poetically captured through color and rhyme!

Bible

For Parent:
Deuteronomy 32:2, "Let my teaching fall like rain and my words descend like dew, like showers on new grass, like abundant rain on tender plants." The picture of "abundant rain on tender plants" is easy to imagine after reading this story selection. Let us be like the tender plants, ready to soak up wisdom and learn from the word of God.

For Child:
Psalm 74:16, "The day is yours, and yours also the night; you established the sun and moon." The story has beautifully captured the day turning to night. The sun is shown with cascading rays after the storm. At night, the gold and silver moon and twinkling stars are almost magical in their look and feel. What a great chance to remind your child that God established the sun and moon. He created them and placed them in the sky and both day and night belong to him!

Language Arts: Early Literacy - Rhyming

Rhyming is a literary choice an author makes when writing a story. This technique is excellent for creating phonological awareness (an early literacy skill). Being able to hear how words go together or come apart and playing with the smaller word sounds will help your child later as they begin sounding out words and learning how to read.

Rhymes often depend upon the ending sound of words within the phrase. For instance, on the first page of the story, "light" and "white" both have the same ending sound. This is not something you have to "teach" your child. Simply hearing you read and listening to the sounds that the rhyming pattern of words make will begin the process in their brain of breaking words into smaller sounds.

Art: Foreshadowing Through Illustration

The title page and dedication page both have hints in the illustrations that foreshadow the rainstorm that occurs later in the story. Foreshadow means to warn or indicate a future event. Before you've begun reading the story, you see the title page. On it is an illustration with flowers, a cat, jump rope, watering can, boot, ball, puddle, and an umbrella. It isn't raining in the picture, but the umbrella is a prominent item in the image. On the next page, you see the inside of a house with an open door and sunlit garden beyond the screen door. Beside the door, two umbrellas stand at the ready. The illustrator shows consistency, forethought, and foreshadowing by including the umbrellas in the illustrations prior to the beginning of the story.

Look at the title page and dedication page illustrations with your child. Ask them what things they notice. If they notice the umbrellas ask them why they are there. See if they can make the connection between the rainstorm later in the story and the umbrellas at the beginning of the book. This type of discussion will help build your child's narrative skills (one of the six early literacy skills; see the introduction to *More Before* for the entire list).

Art: Cotton Clouds

As adults, when we read "cotton clouds," it likely reminds us of cotton balls. Puffy and white, perhaps wispy on the edges. Is your child familiar with a cotton ball? As an exciting art project and a way to make the mental connection between cotton balls and puffy white clouds, have your child experiment with making cotton clouds. Use blue construction paper, glue, and cotton balls. The cotton balls can be pulled apart slightly to make them more loose and airy or pilled upon one another to create a puffy, bright white cloud!

Math: Counting

This story provides many counting opportunities for your child. On the first page of the story, count the garden vegetables in each row, the dogs, or the clouds. Count the clothing and towels hanging on the line. Later in the story, you can count the leaves blowing off the trees, the pigs in the shed, or the ducks and ducklings. Pointing with your finger to each item or letting them point, count the items one by one. This repetitive process will help your child build a solid mathematical foundation for knowing how objects and numbers relate.

Childhood Play: Outdoor Play

The story begins with a sunny day filled with "Singing, swinging outdoor play." Ask your child what they like to play outside on a sunny day. In the illustration, we see a tricycle, a ball, and a girl jumping rope. These options might be included on your child's list of preferred outdoor play activities. Some other options that you can suggest if your child doesn't think of them could be: blowing bubbles, flying a kite, swinging, playing in a sandbox or with a water table, going on a nature walk, collecting rocks, or playing outdoor games like tag or hide-and-seek.

Write down your child's ideas, along with any others that you think of together, and keep the list in a place where you can reference it when outdoor playtime is an option. Having a list of specific ideas can help remind your child of a favorite activity that they might not think of at the moment.

Childhood Play: Indoor Play

Later in the story, a rainstorm blows in and the children have to go inside. Have your child look for indoor toys in the illustrations where the kids are indoors. There's a doll, a spinning top, books, children's artwork (on the wall), a hammer toy, and a ball. Make a list together that includes indoor activities that your child enjoys! Some ideas that might be different from their everyday toys and games could include: making or playing with playdough, drawing, coloring, painting, reading, having a tea party, baking together, and playing with water toys at the sink or in the bath. Having a robust list of your child's favorite indoor play activities to reference can help prevent boredom and reduce screen time!

Science: Weather Changes

As the thunderstorm rolls in we read, "Winds blow bolder. Weather changes. Air grows colder." Later as the storm ends, it says, "Winds shift. ... Sun sneaks back. Warms the air." What we see through the text in both cases is a change or a shift! This is an accurate description of how thunderstorms occur. Warm, moist air rises swiftly and hits cooler areas of the atmosphere. It then condenses and forms clouds and precipitation. This cooled air drops back down and hits the ground with strong winds and the rain. This is just a bit of the scientific side of storms; obviously, your child doesn't need to know this information yet. Pointing out when it occurs in the story (and in your daily lives) how storms are often accompanied by a shift in wind or temperature, will begin to teach your child about the weather and world around them.

Another clue that tells us that a storm might be coming is the color shift of the clouds and sky. The author captures it perfectly throughout the story: the day begins, "White on blue on sunny day." And then as the storm rolls in, "Gray on gray. Dark and glooming. Black on black. Storm is looming." Point out to your child this color shift in the story as the storm starts. It is something they can begin to be aware of in their own world. If it suddenly gets dark and cloudy, there might be a storm coming. That can be a good indication for them to go inside or check with an adult about the weather.

Safety: Thunderstorm Safety

At the beginning of the story, we see all the people and animals outside enjoying the beautiful day. The dogs and cat are running around. The children and mother are outside playing and hanging laundry. The pigs can be seen outside the shed in their pen. The father is plowing the field with the horses looking on. As you read the story together, ask your child where the people and animals go when the storm starts.

See if your child can find the people and animals indoors. In the illustration where the child and dog are under the covers in bed, notice what's happening outside the window. The pigs are under their pen's shelter, and the farmer is bringing the horses into the barn. Later we see the cat inside the barn with the horses looking out at the rain. Talk with your child about how we stay safe during storms. Staying indoors is imperative when there could be lightning, hail, or strong winds. For an older child, this might be a good time to introduce tornado or hurricane safety (if you live in an area that has these weather events).

Art: Ways to Illustrate Rain

The illustrator has done an incredible job of showing rain! Rain—coming down under the clouds in sheets, pouring down through the images in straight lines, dropping in downward arrows that look a bit like a splash, and in droplets. Look through the illustrations with your child and ask them on different pages if it's raining gently or hard. How can they tell? On the page with the pigs under their shed, your child might notice the water pouring out of the gutter into the barrel. This would definitely indicate a hard rain. Later, the droplets are big on the page and more spread out. It looks like it's raining more gently at this point.

Ask your child if they would like to make a picture that includes rain. You can help them reference the illustrations and look at the different ways that this story shows rain. Together you can try imitating the styles in which the illustrator portrayed the rain.

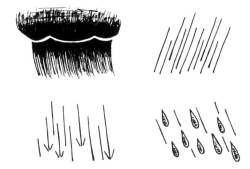

Science: Dirt and Mud

Before Five in a Row and *More Before Five in a Row*-aged children are discovering the world around them! It's likely your child has already played in a dusty dirt pile or squelched their way through a mud puddle. This lesson is a chance to help them make a more meaningful connection in their world—one between dirt and mud. Ask your child if they know how to make mud or where it comes from. If they don't, try to lead them to

the answer. You can ask, "Do we ever have mud in our yard? What about dirt—do we have that? What happens when the dirt gets wet? Let's try it and find out!"

Put a small amount of dirt in a bowl and add a bit of water at a time. Let your child stir the dirt and water to create mud! Then you can show them the picture near the end of the story where the pigs and children are playing in the mud. Explain how that area was probably just a dry, dusty patch of dirt before the rain came and mixed water with the dirt to make the mud. Ask them what will happen when the air and wind dry the mud? Yes, it will become dusty again. Place the experimental mud, still in the bowl, outside in a sunny area and wait for it to dry. Check on it with your child and see how long it takes to turn back to dirt after the water has dried up. This experiment will help your child make a big-picture connection and is also a great sensory experience as well. (Some children will dislike the idea of touching the mud. Providing your child opportunities to feel different textures is a positive way to help them become less reactive to various stimuli.)

Childhood Fears:
Thunder, Lightning, and Loud Noises

Many children are afraid of thunder and lightning or simply don't like the sound of thunder. The children in the story are upset and covering their ears because of the "Pounding, hounding, noisy-sounding" storm.

While this is a common childhood fear, there are some things that you can do to help your child overcome their feelings or aversions:

- Talk about the benefits of rain and why we need it.

- If your child is old enough, explain what

thunder is. Very simply, it is the vibration of air that creates a cracking, booming, or rumbling sound (the vibration is caused by the heat of the lightning or the electricity that passes through the air).

• If your child is too young to explain this to or reason with, distract them with something enjoyable. Watch a movie together, have a tickle fight or a dance party.

• You can also lessen the intensity of the sound by playing music or putting headphones on your child and playing a favorite movie for them.

• Teaching your child basic storm safety can often reassure them and give them a sense of control (see the previous lesson on Thunderstorm Safety).

• Have empathy. Even some adults have anxiety or fears about thunderstorms. Be understanding and compassionate and know that through continued exposure to storms and the knowledge that everything was okay in the end, your child will likely outgrow their fears.

Thunder Cake by Patricia Polacco is a lovely story about a grandmother who has her grandchild help her gather ingredients for a cake as a storm approaches. The cake must go into the oven before the storm reaches them. And then, of course, there's a delicious cake to eat in the end. The grandmother in this story turns something fearful into something exciting and a bit celebratory. After reading this story together, you could ask your child what their favorite "thunder snack" might be. Perhaps making a special thunder treat together could become a family tradition.

Social Studies: Clotheslines

Many children today won't recognize what the mother is doing in the illustration where she's hanging clothes on the line. Explain to your child that before we had electric clothes dryers, people would wash their clothes (sometimes by hand or in a hand-cranked machine) and then

32

hang them on a line outside to dry in the sunshine. Ask them if they think that would be harder than putting them into the dryer and turning it on. Discuss what you would do if it were raining. You'd have to wait to wash your clothes or hang them up inside your house!

Health: Baths, Why and How Often

After the rain, there's mud everywhere! The children and dogs enjoy splashing and playing in the mud. In the next image, you see them carefully washing the dogs. A couple of pages later, the children too are getting baths. Playing outside and getting dirty or sweaty can be lots of fun. It's necessary, though, to bathe and get clean afterward.

Preschool-aged children can be at an age that they begin questioning why they need a bath or why they can't bathe themselves. Talking with your child about why we take baths or showers and how often we should bathe is a great way to begin building your child's personal hygiene perspective and encourage independence. Some points to discuss:

- Bathing helps wash away germs

- Bathing helps keep people healthy

- It makes you look and smell clean

- Baths are relaxing at the end of a long day

- It's fun to have quiet play in the bathtub, pouring water, playing with bubbles, etc.

Teach your child how to take charge of things that they can do themselves during bath time, such as soap up a washcloth and clean their body,

towel dry themselves, and brush their own hair.

Be sure to remind your child that bath time safety is important. They need to let an adult test the water temperature before they get in. They might need help climbing in so they don't slip. The bath isn't a place to stand up or jump around—it can be slippery, and it's always safest to sit while playing or bathing in the tub.

Geography:
Story Location - Farmland and Ocean

You or your child might notice that there is water surrounding parts of the farmland. At the beginning of the story, we see a boat sailing just over the hill from the house. And at the end, with the house up on a cliff, we see a whale! The house, yard, and surrounding land have a familiar farmyard feel that could be located in many areas of the United States or Canada. Even the boat could be sailing in a small lake near a farm. However, when we see the whale, we suddenly realize that this farmhouse is located next to an ocean!

The illustrator, Beth Krommes, lives in New Hampshire. Her location likely influenced the illustrations; New Hampshire, or other east coast states, would have land with nearby ocean similar to what is represented in *Blue on Blue*.

You can point this out to your child and talk about how the east and west coasts of the United States of America have land that is right up against the ocean. If you lived in these areas you could look out your window and see the sea, boats sailing, and perhaps even a whale!

*Have your child place the **Blue on Blue** story disk on the storybook map either on the ocean or house nearby.*

BUNNY CAKES

34

Title:	*Bunny Cakes*
Author:	Rosemary Wells
Illustrator:	Rosemary Wells
Copyright:	1997

Summary

Max and Ruby are both making delicious cakes for Grandma's birthday! Max makes several trips to the grocer with a list from Ruby, to which he adds his own item. The grocer can't read Max's writing, but Max is persistent and finally finds a way to help the grocer understand what he wants.

Bible

For Parent:

Romans 5:2-4, "...and we boast in the hope of the glory of God. Not only so, but we also glory in our sufferings, because we know that suffering produces perseverance; perseverance, character; and character, hope."

Max's perseverance is what eventually gets him the Red-Hot Marshmallow Squirters! Romans 5:2-4 tells us that suffering produces perseverance, which produces character, and finally, character produces hope. There was suffering for Max when the grocer couldn't read his writing and wouldn't give him the squirters. He didn't give up, though; he kept trying different things until he found something that worked.

God knows that we need hope! He has taken something we often encounter in our world (suffering) and made way for that suffering to produce something beautiful in our lives—perseverance, character, and hope!

One scientific and visual illustration of this concept can be found in the emergence of a butterfly or moth from its chrysalis or cocoon. Emerging is not easy for the butterfly/moth. It is a challenge or a struggle for them to work their way out of the chrysalis/cocoon. But through this struggle, their legs are building strength and the blood is pumping into their wings so that when they have fully emerged, they will be stronger and ready to open their wings (to dry) and eventually fly! If someone helps them out of their cocoon and makes it "easier" for them, or takes away their struggle, they won't have the strength or readiness to be what God designed them to be.

The same is true in our lives. Knowing this can help us have a different perspective on the suffering that we experience. James 1:2-4 says, "Consider it pure joy, my brothers and sisters, whenever you face trials of many kinds, because you know that the testing of your faith produces perseverance. Let perseverance finish its work so that you may be mature and complete, not lacking anything."

For Child:
Ephesians 4:32, "Be kind and compassionate to one another, forgiving each other, just as in Christ God forgave you."

For a young child's memory verse, you could shorten it to "Be kind ... to one another, forgiving each other." Or even just, "Be kind ... to one another."

Max wanted to help Ruby in the kitchen but accidentally broke the eggs, spilled the milk, and bumped the flour. Ruby had lots of opportunities to be kind, compassionate, and forgiving towards Max.

As you read the story with your child, point out the moments that Ruby could have said, "It's okay Max, it was an accident. I forgive you."

Helping your child see opportunities to be kind and forgive, both in stories that you read together and in life, will help build their emotional intelligence. If you do this regularly and continue to model kindness, compassion, and forgiveness to your child in your own life, they will begin to respond in the same way.

One effective method for creating empathy in a young child, which often leads to the willingness to apologize, is to have them look at their sibling's or friend's face/eyes when they've hurt them. Seeing the pain or sadness in someone else seems to press a pause button on the offending child's frustration or anger, and break through to their sense of empathy and compassion. This pause in anger and empathy often leads to an authentic apology without much prompting.

You can remind your child that the reason we forgive others (even when we don't want to) is because God forgives us. We see this at the end of Ephesians 4:32, "Be kind and compassionate to one another, forgiving each other, just as in Christ God forgave you."

Art: Illustration - Cover Design

Look at the cover of the book with your child. The cover illustration shows Max inside a large baking bowl, holding an oversized whisk, surrounded by the extra large milk, measuring cup, and eggs. It seems to be an amusing reference to the book title, *Bunny Cakes*—almost as if Max was going to be mixed into a cake.

If you haven't read the story yet, ask your child if they think Max is going to *make* a cake or *be* a cake? Then have a good giggle together, because that's so silly! The illustrator's choice to use a playful perspective, showing Max inside a BIG baking bowl, is a great way to capture the attention of young readers!

Language Arts: Vocabulary - Parts of a Book

This is knowledge for you (the parent) to know and perhaps reference here or there to your child. There are many parts of a book. Each piece has a different name—some might be new to you!

- **Book** - the entire object: covers, pages, etc.

- **Front** - the cover

- **Back** - the opposite side from the front

- **Head** - the top of the book, when held in a reading position

- **Tail** - the bottom of the book, when held in a reading position

- **Spine** - the vertical edge on which the pages are connected

- **Fore edge** - the vertical edge opposite the spine, with unconnected pages

- **Leaves** - the sheets of paper that make up the pages

- **Boards** - the hard front and back covers (these are called boards because they used to be made of wood)

- **Endpapers** or **Endsheets** - the papers that are attached to the hard front and back cover or boards

- **Pastedown** - the endpaper or endsheet that is attached, or pasted down to the board

- **Flyleaf** - the endpaper or endsheet that isn't pasted to the board, but is opposite it

36

Knowing specific names or terms helps us to be able to communicate clearly. For instance, in the Art lesson about endpaper illustrations, you will know where to look to find the art that is being discussed.

Language Arts:
Early Literacy Skills - Print Awareness

Print awareness is one of six early literacy skills that can help a child be ready to learn to read and write (see the introduction to *More Before* for more information on these skills). The other five skills are print motivation, vocabulary, letter knowledge, phonological awareness, and narrative skills. Included in print awareness is knowing how to how to hold or handle a book and how the printed words flow on the page.

Learning to read and write does not begin in kindergarten. Instead, from birth, your child is learning literacy skills through interactions with you, reading together, snuggling and looking at a book, singing songs, and hearing you speak to them.

Young children need to learn that a book contains words, that there is a correct way to hold a book, and how the book works. Is it upside down? Where do we start? Which direction do we read?

One of the best ways you can teach and encourage this knowledge is by reading to your child. They will learn from you the correct way to hold a book. If you occasionally point to words as you read, or run your finger from left to right along with the sentence, they will realize how letters form spoken words, words form sentences, and that we read them from left to right.

Our story provides an excellent opportunity for little fingers to trace letters and practice print awareness.

The slightly larger, handwritten lettering of Ruby's grocery item on the illustrated lined paper (in the bottom corner of the page), is a nice size for your child to trace lightly with their finger. Show your child how to trace the letters with their pointer finger and then let them try.

Art: Endpapers or Endsheets Illustrations

Your child doesn't need to know that the colorful and fun baking pictures that you're going to look at with them are located on the "endpapers or endsheets" of the book. It is just a way to communicate clearly to you (the parent) where exactly you can find these illustrations. (See Language Arts: Vocabulary - Parts of a Book lesson for a full explanation of all book parts.)

The endpapers or endsheets (the papers that are attached to the hard front and back cover or boards) are often the first spread you see when you open the cover of a book. Printed endsheets or endpapers (using a color or illustration) are one way to add an elegant finishing touch to make a book attractive and unique.

With your child, look at the endpaper/endsheet illustrations. Many of the baking items in the story are represented on these pages, but separated, so that each can be seen clearly. This creates a perfect moment to point to and name each item or ask your child to point to an item that you say. Take this opportunity to build your child's vocabulary (one of the six early literacy skills; see the introduction to *More Before* for the entire list) and help them learn the meaning of a new set of words: baking and cooking words!

You could even do this lesson at the kitchen counter, showing your child the "real" baking and cooking items in your own kitchen as you point them out!

The kitchen items shown include:

- Measuring spoons

- Measuring cup

- Teaspoon

- Whisk

- Spatula (a rubber or silicone type for stirring and a metal flat (knife-like one) for spreading frosting or icing)

- Scoop

- Cookbook

- Cake pans or springform pan

- Mixer (with mixing bowl and beaters)

- Sugar bowl (bowl with space for the spoon to stay in the bowl with the lid on)

Baking ingredients:

- Flour

- Eggs

- Sugar

- Milk

- Butter

- Vanilla

Childhood Play: Mud Pies and Earthworm Cakes

Ruby is making Grandma a most delicious "angel surprise cake with raspberry-fluff icing." Meanwhile, Max is making Grandma an "earthworm birthday cake." After reading the book, ask your child why Max is making an earthworm cake outside, instead of baking in the kitchen with Ruby? Ruby is trying to follow a recipe and bake a special cake

and Max wants to help her but isn't quite big enough to help without accidentally making a lot of messes. Outside, Max can be in charge of his earthworm cake. Ruby won't tell him what to do, or *not* do, and he can bake a cake any way he wants to.

Many children's first attempts at "cooking" or "baking" occur outside, perhaps in a sandbox, or with water and dirt. They can practice measuring, pouring, and stirring without fear of flinging bits over the edge of the bowl onto the counter, or dumping ingredients on the floor as Max did. It's actually an ideal way for a child to experiment and learn the basic techniques that we all use to cook and bake!

Mud Book: How to Make Pies and Cakes by John Cage and Lois Long is a playful and inspiring go-along book to read to your child if you want to encourage outdoor "cooking!"

Teaching Tip:
Kinetic Sand™ or playdough make great indoor substitutes for cold weather or rainy day play! The bathtub is another place your child can practice pouring, measuring, and making "bubble cakes."

Sensory Play:
Why Sensory Play is Important

Childhood desires to "pretend cook" and to get dirty are short-lived and will be gone before you know it. Encourage your child in this outdoor, imaginative play! It has many benefits beyond keeping your kitchen clean. The sensory experiences of sifting dry sand, packing wet sand, kneading or stirring mud are actually broadening your child's world. Playing with different textures and talking about them together can build your child's language skills. Suddenly sand

isn't just sand, it's *dry and gritty* or *heavy and wet*!

The practice of measuring, pouring, and stirring that they can do without a worry in an outdoor play space, is not just play—it's building your child's fine motor skills. Learning how to control small muscle groups will help them later on when they learn to tie their shoes, button and zip their clothing, and write!

Finally, sensory play is calming! Children are sometimes bored, agitated, or restless, and this kind of play can be soothing to their senses. Your child may be more peaceful after swinging, jumping, playing in a sandbox, or taking a bath. Each of these activities involves sensory input. Let your kids enjoy a good mud pie baking session outside, followed by a nice warm bath, then sit back and enjoy a bit of calm!

Language Arts and Art:
Writing and Art Tools - Crayon and Pencil

At the beginning of the book, on the two-page spread before the first page of the story, is an illustration of a red and blue crayon and a pencil. These are what Max and Ruby use to write their lists for the grocer. Ruby writes her letters and words in pencil, while Max "writes" in blue and red crayon. One of the times that you read this story with your child, point out the page with the crayons and pencil on it. You can ask if they like using a crayon or pencil more? Which crayon would they prefer to use, red or blue? Or a different color? As you read through the story, point out and show your child where Ruby has written words with her pencil on the list and where Max has tried to write words on the list with his crayons.

Gather a red and blue crayon and a pencil, along with some lined paper (yellow if you want it to match the story). Before reading the story, set out the writing tools and paper at a table where your child is seated. Then open the book to the page showing the crayons and pencil (before the beginning of the story). Pause there and see if your child gets the connection of having the same writing tools that are shown on the page. If they don't notice, you can point out and mention the tools shown on the page and that the same red and blue crayon and pencil are on the table for them to use.

Now you can let your child practice "writing" or drawing using the waxy colored crayons and the lead pencil. We can use both a crayon and a pencil to write and draw with, but is it easier to use one or the other? Which one do they like more? By 3-5 years old, children will have already used a crayon and/or pencil, but this experiment is about trying both tools during the same lesson and discussing the similarities and differences.

Social Studies: Children Want to Help

Most young children want to be helpful! They are excited to be getting bigger and are ready to stretch their wings by trying things that they've seen you do. Just like adults, children need meaningful, purpose-filled work to do and feel proud of.

Max wants to help Ruby bake the cake that she is making for their grandma. Ask your child if they enjoy helping. What's their favorite way to help around the house? Together you and your child could come up with a list of ways that they could help.

Teaching Tip:
In the beginning, giving your kids chores, jobs, or work to do will create more work for you. You will need to show them the proper way to do the job, and they will make mistakes and messes along the way. But in the end, it will be worth all the time and effort that you put into it. You will have children that can actually help you, and they will also be gaining invaluable life skills.

Don't forget that you will need to have a designated place where things belong (and teach your child where this is) if you expect your child to be able to put them away properly.

Here are some common chores that are age-appropriate for a 3-5-year-old:

Indoor Jobs:

- Sweep or run the dustbuster to pick up crumbs (offer a whisk broom if your child struggles with a full-size broom)

- Wipe down the table or chairs with a damp cloth

- Put shoes or clothes in the right place (hook, cubby, drawer, closet, or hamper)

- Clean up toys, books, crayons, etc. after using them

- Get dressed (or help you get them dressed)

- Help set the table (napkins and non-breakable plates/bowls)

- Clear the table after the meal (again, napkins and non-breakable plates/bowls)

- Fold laundry (washcloths, napkins, and kitchen towels make great starters for folding)

- Wipe down cabinets

- Help feed pets

Outdoor Jobs:

- Sweep outside porch/walkway

- Pick up leaves or small sticks

- Weed garden areas (with direction and supervision)

- Put outdoor toys in the right place

Science:
Baking - Mixing Ingredients Together

Baking is a science. It's mixing ingredients and using acid and heat to create a reaction. One way to begin exploring this idea with your child is to ask questions the same way a scientist would! As you read this book (or while you're baking together, if you choose to bake a cake with your child), ask, "Why do you think Ruby mixed up the milk, flour, sugar, and eggs?" Or, "What happens when we put the batter into the oven? What comes out of the oven?"

You can begin some simple explanations about how most recipes for cookies or cakes have flour, sugar, eggs, and butter. These are called ingredients. We mix up the ingredients to form a mixture (called a batter). Then we add heat to cook that mixture. The heat makes the mixture rise and cook ... and we end up with cake! This is, of course, a very simple, beginning discussion about baking. If your child is excited about baking, you can search for cookbooks and recipes (online or in books) designed for young children.

Language Arts: What's in a Name?

Ruby is making Grandma an "angel surprise cake with raspberry-fluff icing!" Wow, that sounds exciting and amazingly delicious! Ask your child if they'd rather have a cake called sponge cake, or one called carrot cake, or an "angel surprise cake with raspberry-fluff icing?" Ask if they think Ruby made up that name. Play a fun game with your child of renaming some cookies and cakes to make them sound more exciting. (You can continue this game with any food. A grilled cheese sandwich, for example, could be called *flame-toasted cheesy triangles*.)

Rename the Food Game
Here's a list below to play with...

lemon cake (example: *tangy yellow zinger cake*)
carrot cake
chocolate cake
peanut butter cookies
sugar cookies
chocolate chip cookies
(add your own!)

Art: Illustrations Telling Part of the Story - Zoom In

Max accidentally knocks the eggs onto the floor, and they break. In this illustration, instead of seeing the kitchen table, Max, and Ruby (the way you do in the picture on the left page) the artist has chosen to "zoom in," focusing on the broken eggs and Max's feet on the floor. This does two things: first, it shows direction—the eggs have fallen down to the floor! It also shows very clearly that the eggs are cracked and broken. The text doesn't say that the eggs fell and broke, it reads, "Don't touch anything, Max,' said Ruby. But it was too late." So the author/illustrator is relying on the picture to help tell that part of the story!

When the milk spills, the picture zooms in again. The focus becomes the milk pouring out of the bottle and down onto the floor. The text here reads, "Don't bump the table, Max!' said Ruby. But it was too late." Without the illustrations, you wouldn't know what had happened. Again, it's the combination of text and picture that clearly relays the story to the reader!

The same illustrative choice, to zoom in, is made again when the flour falls off the table. Down goes the flour, spilling onto the floor. Point out to your child that the flour bag is upside down as well—uh-oh! It's fun to look for this type of attention to detail that an illustrator will choose to include to make a story more realistic.

When you notice this type of illustrative choice (to tell part of the story through the picture), have your child guess what happens with out seeing the illustration.

Early Literacy:
Writing Readiness - Scribbling

Max demonstrates something beautiful in our story: the innocent childhood knowledge that writing communicates something! He knows that by writing words down on paper, someone else can understand what you need/want/think. Most children become aware within their first few years that we are actually communicating something when we write letters, words, and sentences. They will often do exactly what Max does and carefully work as hard as they can to "write" something. Most of the time we (adults) don't even know what they're thinking or writing. But they do!

Max doesn't get discouraged when the grocer can't read his "writing." Instead, he tries writing it a different way and then in the "most beautiful writing he knows." Finally, he has a new idea ... to *draw* a picture of the Red-Hot Marshmallow Squirters he so desires.

Writing readiness doesn't happen when your child starts tracing alphabet letters. It begins when they are strengthening their hands by pushing up from tummy time as a baby. It continues as they push and knead playdough or clay with their fingers, and when they swing on the monkey bars at the playground. It heads even more towards writing when they first grip a crayon in their pudgy toddler fist and scrub it across the paper.

Writing readiness takes off when your child starts "writing" the way Max did in our story. Those scribbly shapes are showing all of the connections they're making between brain and fingers—the link between having ideas and writing them down to communicate them to someone else. They are learning the motor connections and challenges of holding and controlling a writing tool. They're discovering how their movements are making the marks on the paper and how to connect those marks to make shapes and stories.

Teaching Tip:
These scribbles are an essential time of practice **without** expectations! Once you give them actual letters to trace, the expectation to get it "right" can become stronger than the desire to enjoy it. Don't rush your little one. Savor their excitement and know that they are doing the hard work of learning ... but *loving* it because they're free to experiment!

The Write Start by Jennifer Hallissy is a great resource book for discovering activity ideas that will encourage your children as they become little writers. (Most of the book is for older children, but it does include comments about the scribbling stage and early letter formation.)

Art: Viewpoint

In the illustration showing Max getting milk for Ruby at the grocer's, the point of view changes from looking straight at the characters to looking down from a high vantage point. You see the back of the grocer's head and body, the counter, and on the floor looking up at the grocer, you see Max.

Why did the viewpoint change? Perhaps the illustrator wanted to reinforce the idea that Max is little. Ask your child, is Max is big or small? Even a young child will likely see Max as little because of the viewpoint the illustrator chose to use in this picture.

Social Studies: Signs

While Max was at the store, Ruby drew a sign that she posted on the screen door: a picture of Max, with a red circle around him and a diagonal line through the circle. This is the symbol or sign for "no," or *not permitted*. Ruby said, "Max, the kitchen is no place for you," and posted a sign on the door telling Max that he was not allowed to go in.

You can explain this briefly to your child and maybe even have fun making "no _____" signs together. If your child can draw a circle, then they can try to make a "no" sign of their own. Take the time to show your child other signs that you see when you're around town. Some signs you can point out to your child might include, a wordless sign on a bathroom door that shows if it's for men or women, a handicapped sign on reserved parking spaces, a stop sign, or a no parking sign.

Early Learning: Getting New Ideas

How did Max get the idea to draw a picture of the Red-Hot Marshmallow Squirters instead of trying to write the word? Maybe Max got the idea to draw a picture from seeing the sign that Ruby made and posted on the door. Ruby didn't write NO MAX on the sign because Max can't read yet. Instead, she drew a picture of him with the circle and line through it to show him that he wasn't allowed in the kitchen.

A picture is worth a thousand words, or so the saying goes. In the illustration on the page where Max has a new idea, his eyes are looking at the "No Max" sign sitting next to him. He suddenly realizes that he can draw a picture and the grocer will know what he wants! Max is so excited that he runs to the store! Sure enough, as the grocer reads down Ruby's list, he sees Max's drawing and finally understands that Max wants Red-Hot Marshmallow Squirters. Success!

Your child, like Max, is learning new things all the time. They'll learn from watching you, reading books, watching shows or movies, and playing games, just to name a few of the countless learning opportunities they'll have. When you point out things and name them, or show them to your child as you read or run errands, your child will make connections and have new ideas sprouting up constantly. It's so much fun to watch their busy brains think up new ideas!

Art: Search-and-Find

After telling Max to stay out of the kitchen, "Ruby finished up her cake." In the picture showing Ruby in front of the mixer, there's a window behind her. When you get to this page as you're reading the story (if your child hasn't already noticed), ask your child, "Where's Max?" The illustrator has chosen to show Max's ears sticking up outside the window. He's stayed outside as Ruby asked him to, but he's still in the picture, and you can tell where he is if you look carefully. Kids love search-and-find activities, and this is an easy example that even a young child can find if they look for it!

If your child got excited about finding Max, you can search online or at your library for a "look-and-find" book for ages 3-5. There are many options available. These can be great for entertaining children in a waiting room or in the car. In addition, *Max and Ruby Play Hide-and-Seek: Lift-the-Flap Book* by Anne Paradis is a delightful go-along book to read together.

Social Studies: Being Gracious

Grandma was thrilled with both of the cakes that Ruby and Max made for her! Ask your child if they think Grandma is really going to eat both cakes? Would they want to eat an earthworm cake with caterpillar icing? Rabbits don't eat dirt or earthworms, so Grandma is doing something lovely—she's being gracious. Being gracious means that you are kind, courteous, and pleasant. Grandma is making sure that both Ruby and Max feel good about their efforts.

Ask your child about ways that they can be gracious. Daily opportunities that children have to be

kind, courteous, and pleasant often happen at meal times. Young children are frequently being exposed to new foods and flavors. This can be unpleasant for some children. Discuss with your child what gracious things they can say about food that's been lovingly made for them even if it's not their favorite. They don't have to be thrilled like Grandma, but they can politely and graciously say, "That's not my favorite," or, "No thank you." They could also comment on food that they do like, "Thanks for making me the _____ that I really enjoy!" or, "This is delicious! Thank you!"

*Have your child put the **Bunny Cakes** story disk on the storybook map at the Corner Grocer store.*

GO TO SLEEP, LITTLE FARM

46

Title:	*Go to Sleep, Little Farm*
Author:	Mary Lyn Ray
Illustrator:	Christoper Silas Neal
Copyright:	2014

Summary

A little girl and a farm ready themselves for sleep as the day ends. The story's poetic rhythm creates a calming bedtime experience.

Bible

For Parent:

Isaiah 66:13a, "As a mother comforts her child, so will I comfort you..." The last picture in the story is of a mother leaning over her daughter, whispering into her ear. The comfort and peace of that moment are captured perfectly by the illustrator. Imagine, if you will, being wrapped in a warm, gentle hug and hearing whispered words in your ear from God. Whispered words that can relax your spirit and soul. There's a tangible moment, as a mother comforts her child, when the baby or child melts into the comfort of their mother and exhales. God provides that same comfort to you. Take a moment today, a pause from the privilege of comforting others, to be comforted yourself!

For Child:

Psalm 4:8, "In peace I will lie down and sleep, for you alone, Lord, make me dwell in safety." For a memory verse well suited to younger children, you could shorten it to "In peace I will lie down and sleep." You can tell your child that this verse helps us know that God loves them and wants them to relax and go to sleep peacefully.

Science: Insects - Bees

Bees are flying insects that help to pollinate plants and flowers. They make honey and beeswax.

Looking out the window, the little girl in the story sees a bee flying across the skyline. On the following page, the bee "makes a bed in a rose." Bumblebees or wild bees, particularly males, sometimes sleep in flowers. The females tend to return to the hive or their nest at night to work or sleep.

Ask your child if they were a bee, would they enjoy sleeping inside a flower? Where would they choose to sleep? If your child is not familiar with roses, buy one at the store or at least stop to smell the roses next time you see some. If you you're able, let your child feel the petals. Rose petals are silky soft. Don't you think they would make a lovely bed?

If you're playing the Animal Classification Game, create your own card by drawing or cutting out a picture and gluing it to an index card. Or use the bee card provided in the index to add to your collection.

Science: Shadows

The very first illustration upon opening the book is of the little girl holding her teddy bear and looking out the window. The low sun on the horizon (as it sets) streams in the window and casts long shadows on the floor that trail behind her and her bear. There are shadows of the toys on the floor, too. Your young child will not understand what creates a shadow, but by pointing it out and discussing it, you will help create awareness and interest in future science lessons.

You don't have to explain what makes shadows; just look for them with your child and provide opportu-nities for your child to create shadows. Grab a piece of paper, a pencil, and a toy (plastic animal, block, cup, etc.). Go outside and put the object on the ground or up on a block if needed. Place the paper in the area that the light is creating a shadow of the object. Let your child try to trace the outline of the shadow.

Notice shadows with your child at different times of the day. The angle of light distorts true sizes. The little girl's shadow, in the book, is much bigger than she is because of the angle of the sunlight shining on her. In the evening just before dark, or in the early morning, the low angle of the sun will produce longer or "taller" shadows. At noon when the sun is directly overhead, a shadow will appear shorter or disappear.

A lovely poem that illustrates the way a shadow behaves is "My Shadow" by Robert Louis Stevenson, from the book *A Child's Garden of Verses*:

> I have a little shadow
> that goes in and out with me,
> And what can be the use of him
> is more than I can see.
> He is very, very like me
> from the heels up to the head;
> And I see him jump before me,
> when I jump into my bed.
>
> The funniest thing about him
> is the way he likes to grow—

Not at all like proper children,
which is always very slow;
For he sometimes shoots up taller
like an india-rubber ball,
And he sometimes goes so little
that there's none of him at all.

Search online for additional verses if your child enjoys this poem.

Another wonderful resource for introducing your young child to poetry is a DVD called *A Child's Garden of Poetry*. It includes many poems (some famous) read by both children and celebrities. It can be found online to purchase or perhaps through your local library to borrow.

Science: Animals - Beaver

To learn more about beavers, see the Science: Animals - Beaver lesson in *Red Knit Cap Girl and the Reading Tree*.

Science: Insects - Fireflies

As the beaver makes his bed in the bog, fireflies drift and light up around him. Fireflies (or lightning bugs, as they are commonly called), are soft-bodied beetles, some of which can produce bioluminescence (light) from their lower abdomen. They use their lights primarily for mating purposes. They can hold a steady glow or flash.

Fireflies love warm, humid environments and can be found all over the world. North and South America, Europe, and Asia all have fireflies. Fireflies can be located near standing water, ponds, streams, rivers, or lakes. They also live near forests or fields. In the U.S., fireflies are hard to find west of Colorado. Despite having some warm and humid areas, there are little to no fireflies in the western states.

Show your child the fireflies around the beaver and tell them about the small beetle that can flash a tiny light on its body. You can grab a couple of flashlights and play a firefly game at night with your child. Stand far apart in a dark room and turn your flashlights on and off in a flashing pattern like a firefly might.

If you live in an area without fireflies or it's not the right season to view them, search online for videos of fireflies. Seeing the flashing glowing lights drifting above the grass and in the trees is a magical experience!

If you're playing the Animal Classification Game, create your own card by drawing or cutting out a picture and gluing it to an index card. Or use the firefly card provided in the index to add to your collection.

Science: Baby Animals

In the story, we read that a *fox* calls her *pups* home for the night. A baby animal is often called something different than that same animal when it's full grown. You can show your child the fox and her pups and talk about how the adult is called a fox. While the

baby foxes are called pups. They can also be called a cub or a kit. You might point out that, like a fox, a dog's babies are called pups (or puppies) too. Another example in the story is a fawn. The adult animal is called a deer, but when young, is called a fawn.

Let's look at some different animals and what their young are called. A bear's baby is a cub, a cat's baby is a kitten, and a cow's baby is a calf. There are many more examples; this is simply a tiny sampling to discuss with your child and start building a foundational understanding that sometimes animal babies have a different name then the adult animal.

Even human offspring have different names, depending on age: baby, infant, toddler, and child are all names of young human beings.

Note for the Parent:
Adult male and female animals often have different names as well. For example, male deer are known as a buck or a stag, while a female deer is called a doe. This is something that your child will learn later on. For now, just knowing that baby animals are called different names than the adult will be a benefit to their later learning.

Art: Silhouette

On the page where the bee is finding a bed on a rose, the trees and farmer in the background appear black. You can't see color or details on the branches or trunks. The artistic technique of placing something that is void of color and detail against a white or light background is called silhouette. This method shows the outline or shape of the item without any additional details.

A fun and easy way for your child to create a piece

of silhouette art, with your help, is for you to draw a simple tree shape (or animal, or item of your child's choice. It could be a truck, dinosaur, or butterfly). Draw this shape with a white pencil or chalk onto black construction paper. You could also find a black silhouette shape online and print it out. Then cut out the black shape and let your child glue it onto light colored paper.

You can mention the word silhouette a few times (while reading) as you point out the backlit black trees in the story. Most children won't remember the name or what it means; this is simply an introduction to a new artistic technique.

On the page where it says, "Time for a father to turn off the light," the father's silhouette can be seen in the house window.

Art: Cutaway View

A cutaway view is when part of an image is removed to make the internal (inside) visible. In this story, the illustrator has chosen to remove part of the ground to show the mice hiding under the tree roots. Similarly, we can see the worm sleeping in the dirt because of the cutaway view. Later in the story, we can see into the lake, as if there were a glass wall or aquarium that we are looking through. Part of the water has been removed so that the reader can see the fish sleeping in the brook.

You can bring your child's attention to this artistic technique by asking questions. "Can we usually see the worms when they're down in the dirt? No, that's right, because the soil is covering them up! Isn't it interesting how the artist chose to take some of that dirt away in this picture so that we can see the worm?"

Your child doesn't need to know what the technique is called or even try to recreate it (unless they want to for fun). Simply introduce them to the concept of being able to see something that's usually covered up, by removing part of the object.

Art: Thought Bubbles - Dreams

To show the little girl's dreams, the artist has used thought bubbles, a

50

common way of showing a person's thoughts. We read in the story, "Just as dreams flicker near," and see the thought bubbles floating above her head, cloud-like. On the next page, the bubbles drift up, and in some of them, things appear. Because the little girl is sleeping, we can assume that her thoughts are actually dreams! Ask your child what the little girl is doing in this picture. They may say going to sleep, sleeping, or dreaming. You can point to the girl's head and then to the bubbles going up. You might ask, "What do these mean? Maybe they're showing the little girl's dreams coming up out of her head."

Comic strip artists frequently use thought bubbles to show what the character is thinking. Look online for Peanuts (Snoopy and Charlie Brown) comic strips which are filled with thought bubbles and speech bubbles, and sometimes tell a story with minimal text. (It's important to find age-appropriate comics for young children. Always preview materials before sharing them with your child.)

Mo Willems writes simple children's books with comic strip-style illustrations. The Pigeon books, such as *Don't Let the Pigeon Stay Up Late!*, are fun and engage the reader (child) by asking them to help. *Waiting Is Not Easy!* is another Mo Willems book (from An Elephant & Piggie collection) and is a *More Before Five in a Row* selection. Remind your child about thought bubbles (or see if they notice) when you read *Waiting Is Not Easy!*

Drama: Pretend Play Promotes Learning

Acting things out can be an integral part of a child's natural learning process! It allows them to take what they've seen or heard and play with it in an unstructured way that will help them process and retain the new information.

The little girl the story is seen, in her room, acting out how different animals get ready for bed. We read, "Somewhere a beaver weaves a bed in a bog." On the opposite page, the little girl can be seen piling her toys up on her bed, making what looks like the beaver's bed. She has likely observed the beaver's lodge (home), carefully woven with sticks piled high in a mound. She is processing that information through play by acting like a beaver and carefully stacking her toys up in a mound as the beaver does with the sticks.

The little girl is hiding under a blanket on the page that reads "Finds a bed in a log." Her blanket-covered bed looks like the log that the bear is sleeping in on the previous page. Turn the page, and you'll see the girl under her bed like the mice hiding in their beds under the roots.

In all of these actions, the information that she's been exposed to is being processed kinetically (through carrying out physical activities) rather than just through seeing or hearing about something.

Teaching Tip:
As your child sees, hears, or discovers new information (which is daily, hourly, sometimes even minute-to-minute for a 3-5-year-old!), encourage them to act it out! This creates a natural, multisensory approach to learning for your child.

Language Arts: Early Literacy Skills - Phonological Awareness

Phonological awareness is one of six early literacy skills that can help ready a child to read and write. The other five skills are print motivation, vocabulary, letter knowledge, print awareness, and narrative skills. Included in phonological awareness is noticing smaller sounds in words and playing with them.

Rhyming is a fantastic way to practice phonological awareness because it is actually a smaller part of the word, typically the ending sound, that creates the rhyme. In rose, knows, close, for example, it's the "ose" and "ows" sounds that rhyme. While your child likely doesn't realize they are breaking the sounds of the word apart, they are hearing and practicing different *sounds* that are in a word: *r-ose*, *n-ose*, *cl-ose*. This will build their early literacy skills and help them later on as they begin sounding out words and learning how to read.

The next Language Arts: Rhyming lesson provides practical tips on how to help your child be more aware of the rhythm and rhymes that they hear in this story selection.

Language Arts: Rhyming

On a second or subsequent reading of the story, you could exaggerate or isolate the rhyme on a given page for your child. On the page where the bee "makes a bed in a rose," you could say, "Rose, knows, close!"

Exaggerate the rhyme again on the pages with the fawn out the window and the little girl yawning in her bed. You could say, "Gone, on, fawn, yawn."

Your child will enjoy the rhythm or cadence of the rhyming words as you read, but saying the rhyming words next to one another will help them begin to see how that cadence is built.

If your child enjoys and seems to catch on to hearing or saying a rhyming word, make it a game! You can say one or two words, and they can think of a word that rhymes with your words. For instance, you say, "Toy, boy" and they might say, "Joy."

Language Arts:
Zzz's Sleep Association - Onomatopoeia and Idiom

After several readings, of *Go to Sleep, Little Farm*, see if your child has noticed the Zzz's that are near the trees, animals, and pocket after they've gone to sleep. The Zzz's also appear on the front and back cover of the book near the sheep, bear, and tree.

In the English language "catch some Z's" is a common *idiom* (an expression that is not meant to be taken literally). It means to get some sleep.

Zzz's is also an example of onomatopoeia (ahna-mahta-PEA-uh; a word that imitates a sound). The Zzz letters imitate the sound of snoring. Another example is the "owl who *whoo-whoo-hoots*."

Comic strip artists may be the reason we see Zzz's associated with sleeping. Comic strip art has a limited amount of space to represent concepts. Sleeping versus lying down is hard to show without something distinctive to set the two ideas apart.

If you search online for "Charlie Brown comics sleeping" you'll find many images that use the Z or Zzz to represent a cartoon character sleeping. You can share one or two of these comics with your child. Then have them point out the Zzz's in *Go to Sleep, Little Farm* the next time you read it together.

Have your child draw a picture of a person or animal sleeping and add some Zzz's to it as an example of what they've learned in this lesson.

Language Arts: Personification

This book selection is full of personification. Personification is when human characteristics are given to non-human items.

"As somewhere shadows tuck a house in." This line in the story is comparing a house to a child being tucked into bed at night. The house is being tucked in by the shadows. Personification is often used to appeal to the senses of the listener and help them use their imagination to see or feel what they're reading.

There are many, many other instances of personification in this story. A few more that stand out in their uniqueness are, "Somewhere a story goes to sleep in a book," and "Somewhere a pocket sleeps in a skirt." What beautiful ways to give a person-like quality to those items! You can almost see the story snuggling into the pages of the book as it closes for the night, and the pocket relaxing into the skirt and drooping down as it drifts off to sleep.

Of course, your child doesn't need to know what personification is or why it's used. They will, however, benefit from hearing examples of it!

You can ask them questions that help them begin to acknowledge the personification. What does it mean when it says, "shadows tuck a house in"? Who gets tucked into bed at night? Yes, kids do! Do houses get tucked in? No, they don't. (*giggle*, that's silly!) But it sounds nice and is lovely to think about a house getting tucked in for the night just like you do, isn't it?

Early Literacy: Print Motivation and Print Awareness through Search-and-Find

This story provides opportunities to have your little one search for objects throughout the book. You can have them search for specific items as you read the story. Or you can use this activity to encourage their own literacy development by having them get the book and then look on their own for what you suggest or what they might be interested in finding.

Search-and-find activities encourage early literacy. It is a way for children to "read" before they can actually read. When your child is looking for an object in a book, they are learning how to orient or hold the book in the correct position (upright). They are learning how to turn pages by doing so themselves or watching you. This activity can be done with any story and accomplishes two of the six early literacy skills: print motivation and print awareness (see the introduction to *More Before* for the entire list).

Here are some specific ideas that are searchable in the selected story. You can also come up with your own objects to search for in this story or any other books you read with your child. Once they become familiar with this practice, your child will likely initiate their own searches!

You can ask your child to search for the **owl** as you read. The owl silhouette appears on the cover of the book. It's seen again on the ground, above the mice hiding under the tree roots, and on the following page in the window. It can be seen one last time, flying on the page that reads, "All around, dusk turns to night."

On a different reading of the book, you might have your child search for **Zzzz's**. These can be on the front and back cover and throughout the story!

If your child is beginning to recognize letters of the alphabet, you can have them search for the **A, B, C's**. These appear on the blocks in the little girl's room. Some **numbers** appear on the dream page for which your child could be on the lookout. The **horse** appears many times throughout the story, as do the **barn**, **house**, and **tractor**.

Language Arts: Early Literacy - Bedtime Stories

This book's dedication (look on the copyright page or at the back of the book, depending on which edition you have) is from the author Mary Lyn Ray to her mother. It says, "For my mother, who read me across the threshold of night, as the ordinary turned into story, and story into dream." What a beautiful tribute to a mother who did what many parents do every night: read a bedtime story to their child.

Reading bedtime stories to your children isn't just a convenient way to help them wind down and ready their bodies and minds for sleep. It is a way to connect with your child and create wonderful memories. You can discover, through stories, their likes and dislikes, their favorite colors, and their sense of humor, among many other relationship-build-

54

ing things. Reading to your child builds your child's empathy, vocabulary, and communication skills. Listening to a story increases your child's attention span, and it instills a love of books and reading that will benefit them throughout their life.

Teaching Tip:
Reading to your child at bedtime is a great way to take advantage of the environmental factors that will deepen their ability to listen. Your child might be putting off bedtime, and will therefore be more willing, or even begging, to hear one more story! They will also be tired from a day of work and play. This tiredness can help little bodies and brains calm down, which sometimes makes it easier for them to sit still and listen.

Enjoy the bond that reading with your child creates, and rest in the knowledge that it's also building a great educational and emotional foundation in their lives!

*The story disk for **Go to Sleep, Little Farm** can be placed by your child at the farm area of the storybook map.*

IN A BLUE ROOM

Title: *In a Blue Room*
Author: Jim Averbeck
Illustrator: Tricia Tusa
Copyright: 2008

Summary

A wide-awake little girl is helped by her mother to calm and ready herself for sleep. She loves blue and wants to sleep in a blue room, but has to be patient for a special moment that satisfies her desires.

Bible

For Parent:

2 Corinthians 4:18, "So we fix our eyes not on what is seen, but on what is unseen, since what is seen is temporary, but what is unseen is eternal."

Our story begins, "In a blue room…", and yet, the room is quite obviously not blue, but yellow. The narrator and Alice seem to know something that we don't. Alice says she can only sleep in a blue room and is clearly having trouble going to sleep. After many attempts from her mama to help Alice calm herself and get to sleep, we finally are included in the knowledge that the room does indeed become blue, and Alice can drift off peacefully.

There is an *unseen* circumstance that the reader doesn't know about until the end of the story. It seems a perfect representation of our Christian walk with the Lord. God's word proclaims that there is an end to our story that is unseen: heaven.

56

We are supposed to look to heaven and eternity, and fix our eyes on the end of our story as we live our life here on earth. It's so easy to focus on the details of our day. To focus on producing and protecting the life we want to have here on earth. It's so hard to look beyond our daily circumstances and struggles to trust the unseen and focus on it, despite our doubts.

Alice was waiting for the unseen. She knew that her yellow room was temporary, that it would change, and that the peace and rest she was waiting for would come. This life is temporary and the peace and rest you're waiting for are coming. Eternity is coming.

For Child:
Psalm 34:8, "Taste and see that the Lord is good." "Would you like some tea?" Alice's mama asks. After Alice argues that it's not blue, Mama says, "Just taste." She asks Alice to test the experience—to taste the tea to see if it's good. How can she know if the tea is good or not without tasting it?

David wrote Psalm 34, praising God and declaring his goodness after experiencing it for himself. Psalm 34:8 is asking us all to test the experience for ourselves to see that the Lord is good. Notice all the things he has blessed us with. He is good. He loves us, even as sinners. He is good.

We ask our kids to taste and see all the time. Literally, with food, and metaphorically with trying new experiences. We can help them learn God's goodness for themselves by pointing out to them his provision in their lives. If you pray with your kids often for God's help and protection, as he answers those prayers, you might say, "Did you notice how God helped us find your favorite stuffed animal before bedtime? Isn't God good?"

Psalm 34:8 is a short verse that would work well as a memory verse or a fun start/finish game to play with your child. After reading it and saying it to your child several times, you would say, "Taste and see..." and then have them say, "that the Lord is good!" Switch it up and have them start and you finish.

Science: Sleep

Why does Alice need to go to sleep? Why does she have a bedtime? These are questions you might ask your child as you read through the story for the second or third time.

Children often dislike the idea of going to sleep. It means the end of playtime, it is time without you near, and it's dark and quiet. Helping them understand the value of sleep, why our bodies need it, and what it does for us might give them a better perspective on the importance of sleep.

Sleep is a period of rest for our bodies and our brains after a period of activity. It allows our body to heal and our brain to process information that we've taken in. It helps our immune system (which keeps us from getting sick all the time). It helps us build strong bones (adequate sleep is necessary for healthy bone marrow). Rest keeps our heart healthy. All people and animals need times of sleep for their bodies to work and stay well. (If you've read *Baby Bear Sees Blue* with your child, remind them that Mama and Baby Bear rested and slept after their long day together.)

Sleep is especially important for children. Children are growing physically and mentally at a rapid rate and need quality sleep to allow their bodies time to release growth hormones and make neurological pathways between the information they've received during their awake time.

Talking with your child about the important things that their body does while asleep is a great way to encourage healthy habits and teach them why sleep is so important.

We'll talk more, later on, about some ways to help make the transition to sleep more natural and pleasant for your child.

Science: Five Senses - Smell

Mama brings flowers into Alice's room in preparation for bedtime. Alice laments that the flowers aren't blue, her favorite color. Mama says, "Ah... but smell." Not only does the gentle scent of the flowers act to calm Alice, but her deep breath allows her body to begin slowing down.

Deep breathing can calm the nervous system and help to quiet the mind. Alice's mama brings flowers in as a way to create a calming breathing opportunity. Using certain scents is an excellent option for promoting a peaceful atmosphere for your child at bedtime. Lavender, chamomile, bergamot, jasmine, rose, and sandalwood are scents known to help foster relaxation and sleep. There are many types of scented products available: candles, bubble bath, lotion, diffusers and calming sprays could be used for your child's bedtime routine.

Another way to playfully help your child focus on their breathing and begin the calming down process is to have them give their favorite stuffed animal a gentle ride. While your child is lying in their bed, place teddy or their lovey on their belly and have them inhale deeply, allowing their stomach to fill with air. This will push their stuffed buddy up, up, up, and then have them exhale slowly to lower it back down. Talk them through this cycle several times until they begin to calm themselves and slow down.

Doing this before story time might allow them to lie more calmly as you read. Or breathing together with the lights dimmed, before you leave, might be an enjoyable way to end your evening together.

(The five senses are also covered in science lessons for *Baby Bear Sees Blue*.)

58

Science: Five Senses - Taste

Alice is now in bed, but not yet ready to sleep. Mama brings a cup of tea to Alice and asks her to "just taste" it. Alice sips it and rubs her eyes. After reading it a time or two, you might ask your child, "What do you think Alice tastes?" They might say oranges or tea. The story tells us, "orange tea cools in a brown cup." Guessing that the tea is flavored like oranges would be a valid assumption. Or it could just be an herbal tea that is orange in color. You can ask your child if they would prefer a warm or cool drink before bed.

Ask your child if they like tea. If they haven't had tea, take this opportunity to make a cup of tea for them. A bit of sugar (or honey for children over 1) can sweeten it and make it more enjoyable. You can add ice or milk to cool it to comfortable drinking temperature. If adding milk, shake your milk gallon before pouring; this will create a foam that will rest on top of the tea. Adding a few colored sugar sprinkles on top of the milk foam can make an extra special treat that will undoubtedly become a frequent request.

As Alice drinks her tea, the warmth is calming to her body, while the flavor of the tea causes her brain to focus on what she's tasting and not any racing thoughts that might be keeping her awake. The tea-sipping moment acts like a time-out for Alice's body and brain, allowing her body to relax and calmness to take over.

Warm milk or chamomile tea have long been recommended as remedies to aid asleep. Milk contains an amino acid called tryptophan. Once consumed, tryptophan is converted into melatonin, which helps maintain the body's natural sleep cycle. Chamomile tea acts as a sleep inducer because of the presence of the flavonoid apigenin.

Bananas contain plenty of magnesium and potassium, both of which promote muscle relaxation. A pre-bedtime banana smoothie, for your child, would be a great way to fend off those late-night snack requests while encouraging relaxation and sleep.

Banana Smoothie
1/2 small banana
1 cup milk, almond milk, or dairy-free milk of choice
optional 1 TBS nut butter or sunflower butter
optional 2-4 ice cubes (not too cold or icy, before sleeping)
Blend, serve, enjoy.

Bedtime Tea
Chamomile or caffeine-free tea
Milk or dairy-free milk (added to cool to appropriate temperature)
optional colored sprinkles on milk foam
See above lesson for sweetening and serving suggestions.

Science: Five Senses - Touch

Alice is calming down and lying down, but is still awake. Mama brings in yet another sensory experience to help Alice go to sleep. "It's silky-soft and warm," Mama says as she lays an extra quilt on top of Alice and urges her to "touch." Our sense of touch is a powerful tool that can help us unwind.

As you read the story with your child, ask them what Alice might be feeling when Mama brings her the extra blanket. Practice, with your child, noticing differences through touch. "Is your stuffed animal silky or rough? Are your sheets warm or cool? Does your blanket feel heavy or light?" Questions like these will help your child focus on the sensory input they are receiving, which will shift their focus from worries or the excitement of the day to something specific and unemotional.

Mama likely knows another benefit of the added quilt she brings to Alice. The weight of an extra blanket on your body is similar to a hug or human touch. Hugging releases oxytocin, a chemical that promotes stronger connections between people and makes us feel good. Human touch lowers blood pressure and reduces cortisol (our stress hormone). Providing added weight in the form of an extra-heavy quilt or blanket (or a weighted blanket that you purchase) can provide your child with the calming benefits of deep pressure touch even after you leave the room. (This is similar to holding or swaddling a baby as a way to help calm their nervous system.)

Every child is different, and many will respond well, and calm quickly with the deep pressure of a heavy blanket or quilt. But some will want only a sheet or a very light blanket. Asking your child questions about how things feel to them and what they prefer will give you valuable information in your quest to help create calming sleep routines for them.

Science: Five Senses - Hearing

Incorporating sound into a bedtime routine brings into play yet another of our senses: hearing. Babies in particular often sleep better with white noise. They have spent nine months in the womb, which some research suggests is about the same loudness as a lawnmower is to us. Entering our world can be a shock to their system, uncomfortably quiet, and unfamiliar. For older children, white noise, quiet music, or the soft chime of something like Alice's lullaby bells, can help distract them from less familiar sounds that might disturb them.

If you consistently use white noise (static, rain, gurgling brook, etc.) to help encourage sleep, it has the added benefit of becoming a positive sleep cue for your child. It can be used in hotels or when visiting family or friends and provide a consistent sleep association that can help your child calm and fall asleep more easily.

If your child is not a baby, you can ask them what sounds might be comforting or relaxing to them. Sound machines are readily available and have white noise, music, or nature sounds. Other ways you can provide white noises without having to purchase anything, are to leave a small fan running in your child's room or set a stereo, boom box or alarm clock radio to a static station (easy to find in the AM stations).

Alice's mother knew that the soft chime of the lullaby bells would be comforting and relaxing for Alice and would help her fall asleep. Some children, on the other hand, may prefer a quieter room when drifting off to sleep. As a parent, you know your child and are the best person to help them find what they need to unwind and drift off more easily.

Science: Five Senses - Sight

Our story's crescendo and illuminating moment happens when Mama clicks off the light ... and suddenly, the moonlight floods into Alice's room. Everything is transformed by its pale blue light. The yellow room, flowers, tea, quilt, and bells all appear blue. The moment Alice has been waiting for arrives, everything is blue, her favorite color. And Alice is finally asleep, in her blue room.

Ask your child what their favorite color is. Would they like it if their whole room looked pink, blue, green or whatever that color might be? What do they enjoy looking at while going to sleep? Maybe it's a favorite picture or nightlight. Perhaps it's a stuffed animal or blanket.

Saying goodnight to each item in your child's room can be an enjoyable transition from wake to sleep. Consider adding this goodnight game after reading together and maybe a song or two, whatever your bedtime routine involves. The process of looking at each item and saying goodnight to it allows your child an extra minute or two to process the coming separation from you, as you leave the room.

Goodnight Moon by Margaret Wise Brown is a famous bedtime story about a bunny who says goodnight to everything around him. There are excellent lessons to go with *Goodnight Moon* in *Before Five in a Row*. If you haven't read this story with your child, take this opportunity to get it from the library and read it together.

Health: Stress Reduction - 5 - 4 - 3 - 2 - 1 Calming Technique

Alice's mother helps her calm down through the use of her five senses. As we have been discussing, using our senses brings us into the moment, and helps us focus on something unemotional. The 5 - 4 - 3 - 2 - 1 calming or coping technique incorporates the five senses and is a reliable tool to keep in your parenting toolbox. It can be used at night to wind down or as an alternative to time-out. You can use it for yourself, or your child, if either one of you struggles with anxiety. It can act as a grounding stress reducer by bringing you or your child back to the present through your five senses.

To begin, take a deep belly breath (a breath that causes your stomach to expand like a balloon) then ...

5) Look - Look around for 5 things you can see and name them. (I see my shoes, I see the couch, I see a doll, etc.)

4) Touch/Feel - Notice your body and pay attention to what you can feel through it and name 4 things that you feel. (I feel the chair under me, I feel the warm socks on my feet, I feel the ground under my feet, etc.) For small children, an alternative option is to find 4 things they can physically go touch or feel (I can feel this pillow under my fingers, I can touch/feel the water running from the faucet, I can feel my mom's hair as I stroke it, etc.)

3) Hear - Listen for what you can hear and name 3 things. (I can hear my tummy grumbling, I can hear the TV on downstairs, I can hear the sound of traffic, etc.)

2) Smell - Name 2 things you can smell. Or if there aren't distinct smells, name your 2 favorite scents.

1) Taste - Say 1 thing you can taste. It might be toothpaste from brushing your teeth or orange from the fruit you ate. If you can't taste anything, say your favorite flavor or things that you enjoy tasting.

You can practice this activity often, even as a car or waiting room game, with your child. The more familiar they are with going through the list, the easier it will be for them to use this tool to bring them back to the moment if they do encounter a stressful situation or become anxious. Even just anger or frustration can often cloud a child's judgment and cause them to make poor choices. This technique could also be used instead of a time-out (with your calm presence and guidance), to help them regroup and gain their composure until they're ready to go back to their play.

62

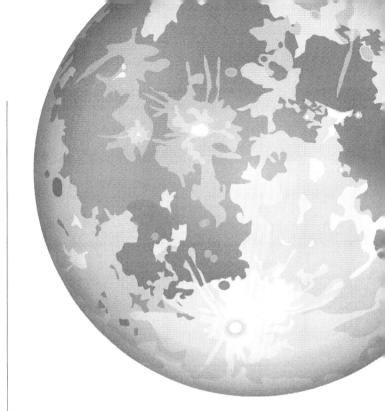

Science: Moon and Earth

Near the end of our story, we see the moon, and on the next page, we see a house sitting on the earth, with the moon out beyond it, in space. While the scale of Alice's house sitting on the earth's surface is certainly not accurate, it does provide a different view then we're used to seeing. Typically in illustrations, we'll see the moon out the window (like we do earlier in the story), or the moon in the sky above the trees or a house (as we see it in the previous illustration). Rarely will you see the moon and earth as if you were on a spaceship or further out in space looking towards them. You can show your child how the moon is in space, far from earth and Alice's house, but it is reflecting light back at earth.

Here are a couple of interesting things about the moon that you can share with your child.

- The moon does not produce its own light but seems to glow because it is reflecting the sun's rays.

- It seems to travel with us or "follow" us when we're walking or driving, because we are traveling a short distance on earth and the moon is in a vast sky above us.

(The moon is discussed further in the Science: The Night Sky - Moon lesson from the book *Waiting Is Not Easy!*)

Math: Counting Backwards 10 to 1

Blast Off is a fun counting game you can play with your child when discussing the moon. It incorporates basic counting and reverses sequencing with large motor movement. Have your child act like a space shuttle, squatting down on the floor and counting down backwards from 10 to 1. After 1, together you'll shout "blast off," and they'll jump as high into the air as they can. You can do the actions with them or just help with the counting. (This idea is also suggested in the Pretend Play: Journey to the Moon - Blast Off! lesson for *Waiting Is Not Easy!*)

Art: Colors

Our story has so many beautiful colors presented in the details and shown in the illustrations. White flowers, orange tea in a brown cup, red and green blankets, yellow bells on a black string, and finally the highly anticipated color blue.

Use your reading time to play a fun color game with your child. Have your child pick a color from the list below and point out all the things in each picture of that color. On the first page of the story, if your child is searching for white, they might point out the lamp, the pillow and sheet, the coloring paper on the floor, and the moon outside the window. Pick a different color each time you read, or for each page, and enjoy a game of color search-and-find with your child!

white
orange
brown
red
green
yellow
black
And finally ... blue

Art: Look/See and Replicate

For an older child, have them choose an illustration that they enjoy. Have them sit down with the picture next to or in front of a blank piece of paper, and provide crayons or markers (with enough colors to be able to replicate the colors in the illustration).

Have them really look at the picture and try to draw it on their paper. If your child seems stuck, you can help them by asking questions like, "What colors do you see?" or "Are there any shapes or lines in that picture that you can draw?"

Encourage your child to observe the details in an illustration, then give them the chance to practice copying it. This activity will help build your child's observational skills. Looking at the techniques and trying to recreate them will help your child learn more about art: line, design, color, and composition, just through observation. This is a lovely way to build their art knowledge and practice new skills at a young age, without the pressure (or expense) of formal lessons.

Teaching Tip:
A young child's re-creation will be very rough. If some of the general colors are included and perhaps a line here or there, that is great! This is not an activity to push for any specific expectations to be met. This is a starting point for helping a child look and see something and then translate that vision (in any way they can) back onto the paper. You can also help them begin to notice specific colors, lines, or shapes by pointing them out in pictures as you read books together. You might say, "Did you notice how that flower has a long straight stem?", or "The blanket on the bed has lines that go this way and that way and cross each other."

64

Drama: Sequencing and Acting Out the Story

One way to help strengthen your child's memory is to play sequencing games. Acting out a story after you've read it several times is a natural way to practice sequencing. Ask your child if they want to pretend to be Alice, or would they like to be Mama? You play the other part.

Alice can pretend to bounce wide awake...
Mama can bring in the flowers...
Alice will pretend to smell them, breathing deeply...
Mama can come with tea...
Alice will take a sip and rub her eyes...

Continue acting your way through the story. Switch roles ... your child will likely find it amusing to be the mother and have you acting out the child's part. If it's challenging to remember the order, in which things occur in the story, you can keep the book nearby and flip through the pages as you act it out. You could even use this as a bedtime game to help your child settle down and relax through play.

*Have your child place the story disk for **In a Blue Room** on the storybook map at Alice's house, under the moon.*

LITTLE BEAR'S LITTLE BOAT

Title: *Little Bear's Little Boat*
Author: Eve Bunting
Illustrator: Nancy Carpenter
Copyright: 2003

Summary

Little Bear has a little boat that he loves. He loves sailing in it and fishing from it until he outgrows it. What is a bear to do without a boat, and what is a boat to do without a bear? In the end he finds a perfect solution to his problems.

Bible

For Parent:

Proverbs 31:26, "She opens her mouth with wisdom, and the teaching of kindness is on her tongue."

We find these descriptions in a long list of attributes about a woman who fears the Lord, often referred to as the "Proverbs 31 woman." "She opens her mouth with wisdom, and the teaching of kindness is on her tongue" comes to mind when thinking about how Mother Bear kindly teaches Little Bear about life changes and how he is growing bigger. The fact that he takes to heart what she teaches him, and goes on to share that knowledge with the bear he gives his boat to, shows that her way of teaching him allowed him to learn and grow! What incredible opportunities we, as parents, are given to be able to teach and instruct our children.

For Child:

Luke 19:2-4, "A man was there by the name of Zacchaeus ... He wanted to see who Jesus was, but because he was short he could not see over the crowd. So he ran ahead and climbed a sycamore tree to see him, since Jesus was coming that way."

What a great Bible story example to share with your child, alongside the Science: Problem Solving lesson below.

Zacchaeus has a problem. He is short and can't see Jesus over the taller people crowded around him. You might ask your child, "What was Zacchaeus trying to do? Why couldn't he see Jesus? What did he do to solve his problem?"

Share with your child that God cares about our problems! He takes care of us and wants to help us. God cared about Zacchaeus too! The tree was already planted and had grown tall before Zacchaeus even knew he would need to climb it. God provided a solution to his problem.

Health: Growing - The Right Fit

Have your child get a pair of her shoes and a pair of your shoes and place them near each other on the floor. Ask your child which shoes are little and which shoes are big. Which shoes will fit her and why? Yes, the little shoes will fit her because she is little. Ask her what will happen when her feet get bigger. That's right, those shoes won't fit her anymore. Why not? Yes, because they'll be too small.

Little Bear has a special boat! It's just the right size for him when he's a small bear. But then what happens? He outgrows it! Discuss with your child how finding things that fit when we're little or big

is important. Shoes and clothing need to fit well to look nice and protect our feet. If shoes are too small or too big, you can get blisters. If clothes are too small they hurt or might look funny. If they're too big what happens? They can fall off, or trip you when you try to run.

Science: Living vs. Non-Living Things

Little Bear gets bigger and bigger. He grows! His boat, however, stays the same size. It doesn't grow. Why? Ask your child if the boat can grow bigger. Why not? Ask them what they do to grow bigger? Eating and sleeping are two things that help us grow. Can a boat eat or sleep? No, why not? Their answers might include, because it doesn't have a mouth or because it's not a person. This discussion is helping your child to think about, and begin to understand, the difference between living things (people, animals, plants) and non-living things (such as boat, bicycle, toy).

Talk together about what things can grow and get bigger. Now, which things can't grow? This talk can lead to discussing which things your child might outgrow. Clothes, shoes, tricycles, toys, sippy cups, toddler plates or utensils, and other things that you think of together.

If you have clothing items saved from when your child was a baby, get an outfit (the smallest you have) and let them see how tiny they were. Talk about how much they've grown and what they can do now that they couldn't do when they were a baby! Growing bigger is an important part of life. Little Bear learns this truth and ends up embracing it and finding a way to bless another little bear in the process.

Social Studies:
Recycle, Reuse, or Donate Items for Others to Use

After talking together about what things your child might outgrow (from the Science: Living vs. Non-Living Things lesson), you can ask them what idea Little Bear comes up with to allow his little boat to continue being used and loved. Yes, he finds another little bear that fits in the boat and gives it to him to enjoy! Ask your child what they can do with things that they've outgrown.

Sometimes there are ways to recycle or repurpose things and continue enjoying them. There's a great go-along book called, *I Had a Favorite Dress* by Boni Ashburn, illustrated by Julia Denos. In it, a little girl outgrows her favorite dress … and then what is she to do? Her mother helps her figure out how to repurpose and continue enjoying her favorite dress in new ways!

Other times we can find someone that could enjoy or use a favorite item that we can no longer use. Just like Little Bear, we can give a favorite toy that we're too big for to a friend. Or we can donate it to a store or organization that will help it get to someone who could use it.

Transportation: Boating - Activities

There are many enjoyable ways to make use of a boat. Ask your child how Little Bear used his boat. He rowed it around the lake, he fished from it, and he lay back and floated in it while dreaming. Which activity your child would choose if they had a boat?

Boats are also a type of transportation. Ask your child if you can use a boat on land? No, that's silly, isn't it? Where would you use a boat? That's right, on the water. Can you drive a car on the water? No, not unless there's a bridge. Boats are a particular type of vehicle that you can use on the water to get from one place to another.

Social Studies: Taking Care of Your Things

Look together at the illustration when Little Bear's mother calls him in for bed. The text says, "he pulled his little boat up to the shore." The

picture shows the boat tied up to a tree on the land. Discuss with your child why Little Bear pulled his boat up and tied it to the tree. What might happen if he didn't tie the boat up? Yes, it might drift away into the lake. Talk about how Little Bear is taking good care of his boat. Ask your child how they can take care of their own things? Make a list together of your child's favorite items and what they can do to care for them. It might look like the examples below:

- Clothes - put them in the laundry basket to be washed

- Toys - put them away at night, so they don't get lost or broken

- Tricycle - park it in the garage, so it doesn't get rusty outside

Your child can illustrate the list, if they desire, by drawing simple pictures of their toys or clothes next to each item listed.

Science: Floating and Sinking

Your child might notice, or you can point out, that the boat floats on the water until Little Bear gets too big for it. Why does it sink when Big Bear tries to get into it? Because he is too heavy for the little boat! While it's too early to fully explain buoyancy to your child, they can observe and learn from a hands-on experiment. You will need aluminum foil and some pennies.

Fold a simple boat out of the foil. Have your child place it in a sink or bowl filled with water. Notice together if it floats or sinks. Now, have your child put a penny in the boat. Add pennies slowly one at a time until the boat sinks. Explain that eventually, the weight of the pennies are too much for the boat

to hold and still continue to float. The little boat in the story could float and hold Little Bear's weight, but when he grew and became a big bear, he was too heavy, and the boat sank.

Social Studies: Explaining Changes to Your Child

Childhood is full of changes. Children can have a hard time accepting those changes if they don't understand what's happening. Explaining what is happening to your child, and why, will help them successfully navigate the change, loss, or new experience that they are facing. In this story, Mother Bear explains how little bears are meant to grow bigger and bigger, while a boat will always stay the same size. While Little Bear is sad, his mother's gentle explanation and empathy give him the reference he needs to move forward and find a way for the little boat to continue being loved and used.

Little Bear truly understands what his mother teaches him about bears growing and boats staying the same size. We know this because, after finding another little bear to give his boat to, he carefully shares this knowledge with him. This other little bear now has an expectation that is realistic and will allow him to enjoy the little boat but also understand that eventually, he'll no longer be able to use it.

It's always good to remember that children don't have the same point of reference that adults have. While something might seem obvious to an adult, like a child outgrowing a beloved tricycle, it's not obvious to the child. What an amazing opportunity parents have to lovingly teach their children about the daily changes that take place in their world!

Art: Illustrations - Same but Different

After reading *Little Bear's Little Boat*, you'll notice that there are two parts of the story that are the same. Little Bear at the beginning is rowing his boat around the lake, fishing from the boat, and lying back and dreaming in it. At the end of the book, Big Bear sees the little bear doing the same three things. The illustrations are very similar but with some differences.

Show your child the first three pictures of Little Bear in his little boat and then the three pictures of the little bear at the end of the story in the little boat. What things are the same in the illustrations and what things are different? Talk about why the pictures might look different. Having distinct changes helps us know that its a different bear using the boat!

Science: Animals - Beaver

To learn more about Beavers, see the Science: Animals - Beaver lesson in *Red Knit Cap Girl and the Reading Tree*.

If you're playing the Animal Classification Game, create your own card by drawing or cutting out a picture and gluing it to an index card. Or use the beaver card provided in the index to add to your collection.

Science: Animals - Otter

Otters are carnivorous mammals that can move quickly on land or in water. They have webbed feet which help them swim and a long tail that propels them through the water. They live in both freshwater habitats (river otters) as well as saltwater ocean habitats (sea otters). They are known to be social creatures and are often seen playing together in the water.

If you're playing the Animal Classification Game, create your own card by drawing or cutting out a picture and gluing it to an index card. Or use the otter card provided in the index to add to your collection.

Science: Animals - Great Blue Heron

The great blue heron is an enormous wading bird. It has long legs, a

long beak, an S-shaped neck, and a massive wingspan of 5.5 to 6.5 feet. It is slate blue-gray in color with a lighter throat and almost white face. Show your child the illustration that includes the great blue heron. The long legs, neck, and beak allow the heron to wade along the shoreline and forage for food. Wading birds will often stand motionless for extended periods waiting for prey to come near them. While flying, a great blue heron's long legs will extend straight out behind him past his tail feathers.

If you're playing the Animal Classification Game, create your own card by drawing or cutting out a picture and gluing it to an index card. Or use the great blue heron card provided in the index to add to your collection.

Science: Flight - Bird's-Eye View

When Big Bear is searching for a little bear, he walks around the lake. He asks Beaver and Otter if they've seen any little bears around, but they haven't. Blue Heron, however, saw a little bear on the other side of the lake earlier that morning! Ask your child how Blue Heron might have seen that other little bear, all the way on the other side of the lake. If your child doesn't know, you can try to steer them towards the answer. You might ask, "What kind of animal is Blue Heron? A bird, yes! What can birds do that Big Bear, Beaver, and Otter can't do? Fly, yes! Do you think Blue Heron saw the other little bear this morning when he flew across the lake?"

Ask your child if they could see more things if they were up in the air like a bird. You can tell your child about the term "bird's-eye view" and how this means seeing things from up above, like a bird might see when it's flying. Looking out the window of an airplane would give a similar kind of view, as would looking down from the top of a very tall building.

Social Studies: Problem Solving

Sometimes we have problems that we need to solve. Ask your child what problem Little Bear encounters in the story. Yes, he outgrows his boat. What can we do when we have a problem? Give up, get help, or figure out a way to fix it ourselves. What does Little Bear choose to do?

He realizes that giving his boat to another little bear will bring joy to someone else and allow the boat to continue to be used. He looks until he finds another bear to give it to. He also chooses to explain what he has learned about bears growing and boats staying the same size, so that the littler bear knows what to expect and what to do when it happens—find yet another bear who's small enough to use the boat.

Little Bear also has another solution to the problem of outgrowing his boat. Ask your child, "What does he do, as a Big Bear, to solve his problem?" Yes, he builds himself a big boat! What a great solution!

Discuss with your child what kinds of problems they might encounter regularly and how they solve them. You could make a list together of the problem and the solution. Sometimes the answer is something they can do on their own and sometimes it's accomplished by asking for help!

Language Arts: Go-Along Book

If your child enjoyed this story and would like to hear more, there is a sequel titled *Big Bear's Big Boat* by Eve Bunting.

*Huckleberry Lake is the perfect location for your child to place the **Little Bear's Little Boat** story disk.*

72

Title: *Mighty, Mighty Construction Site*
Author: Sherri Duskey Rinker
Illustrator: Tom Lichtenheld
Copyright: 2017

Summary

It takes a mighty crew of construction trucks to complete a large building job. Through cooperation and using their individual talents, they end their day tired but proud of the work they've accomplished!

Bible

For Parent:

Luke 1:78-79, "...because of the tender mercy of our God, by which the rising sun will come to us from heaven to shine on those living in darkness and in the shadow of death, to guide our feet into the path of peace."

The sunrise at the beginning of the story, with light streaming outward, brings this verse to mind. The metaphor of the rising sun (being Jesus) coming from heaven to shine on those in darkness and death is such a powerful way to help us imagine the distinct difference of life with or without Jesus. Without him, we are living "in darkness and in the shadow of death"! When he comes to us from heaven, his light will stream into our lives, bringing warmth, life, and light "to guide our feet into the path of peace." Wow, can you feel the difference between these two pictures? What a beautiful promise to remember when you see a sunrise!

For Child:

Lamentations 3:22-23, "The steadfast love of the Lord never ceases; his mercies never come to an end; they are new every morning."

For a young child, you can help them remember, "his mercies ... are new every morning."

Mercy is showing compassion or forgiveness to someone who's done something to you that you could punish. Talk with your child about how we all make mistakes. Sometimes we hurt other people's feelings, or we don't obey, or we're not kind. When we say we're sorry, God forgives us! Just like Mommy and Daddy forgive you because we love you so much, even when you make bad choices, Jesus forgives us too. Because he loves us so much, he forgives kids, mommies, daddies, everyone.

You can mention how it's nice that we all get a fresh start each morning. It's a new day! Just like the trucks in the story, we get to wake up, stretch, and enjoy the day ahead.

Another great Bible verse that's short enough for a memory verse and goes with the theme of the story, is Proverbs 16:3, "Commit your work to the Lord."

Health: Morning Routine

The trucks seem to have a morning routine. After reading the story once or twice, ask your child what the trucks do each morning to get ready. If they can't remember, turn to the page and let them look at the pictures.

Having a routine is beneficial to your child's health. It gives them comfort and helps them feel safe, which reduces stress levels. They know what to expect, and it can help them learn how to handle parts of their life. As they find success in easier routines that you help them put in place, they're able to tackle harder challenges.

Having morning and nighttime routines that include bathing and brushing teeth will help your child develop lifelong personal hygiene and good health habits. A good routine can also help extinguish power struggles. It establishes expectations and allows you to help your child achieve the predetermined goals.

Below is a list of the things the construction trucks do each morning to prepare for their day. Next to each item is something your child could do to be like the trucks!

- Stretch - stretching exercises

- Wipe faces - wash face and brush teeth

- Fuel up - eat a good breakfast

- Greet the sun - morning prayer

- Rev up and run - get going with your day's activities

Health: Stretching

The trucks start out their day by stretching. Stretching increases blood flow to the body and the brain! It's a great thing to add to your child's morning routine and will help ready their bodies for a day of learning and play. Doing some stretches with them can be an excellent way for you to start the day too! You can look up kids' stretches online.

The book *From Head to Toe* by Eric Carle is an entertaining board book for preschoolers that encourages stretching through imitating animals' actions.

Science: Sleep Patterns - Waking to Sunlight

Each truck in the story wakes up when the sun rises. Ask your child to tell you about when they sleep. Do they sleep in the daytime or just at night? Does the sunlight wake them up in the morning?

Light tells our brains that it's time to wake up! Exposure to early morning light, between 6 a.m. and 8:30 a.m., has been scientifically proven to help your body set its internal clock. This body clock is what enables you to feel tired and ready for sleep at night and ready to wake up in the morning! A half-hour of outdoor sunlight in the morning is the most beneficial for setting, or resetting, your biological clock.

Art: Blueprint or Plan

A blueprint is a print of plans (typically designed by an architect) used to build something. It's either white print on a blue background or blue print on a white page. The plan that's unrolled to show the crew of trucks what to do is a blueprint of a large building.

Ask your child why the trucks might need plans to follow? Would they know what to do without plans? You can explain to your child that having building plans might be similar to having a grocery list. If you go to the store without a list, you won't know what you need to buy to be able to make meals for your family. Without building plans, the trucks won't know what each of them needs to do to complete the building.

Sit with your child and let them draw the plans for their day! For example, their plans might include (pictures representing) meals, playtime, errands in the car, an evening bath, and bed. If you have large paper (tabloid size or on a roll), let them make their drawing on a big paper that they can roll up and unroll like the blueprint that the trucks follow. You could also tape several pieces of paper together to make a large one.

Art: Tire Tracks - Printmaking

(See the Art: Parts of a Book lesson from the *Bunny Cakes* unit for a more detailed description of endpapers.)

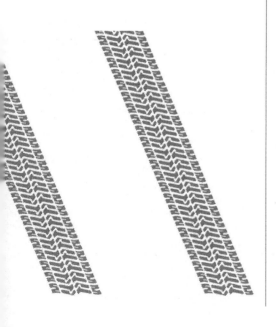

When you open the book, you'll first see two dark yellow pages (the endpapers) with lighter yellow tire tracks running over them in different directions. The tire tracks are tracks that different construction vehicles would make. This simple addition to the artwork is not another picture of the outside of a truck, but instead, a particular piece of information (tire tread pattern or tracks) that we know goes with the trucks.

Ask your child what happens when they step in mud and then walk across the floor? They might say, "It makes dirty prints or tracks." That's right! The same thing happens when a car or truck drives through the dirt and then across the road. It leaves tracks or prints.

If you have toy cars or trucks, you can get some washable acrylic paint and let your child drive the vehicles through the paint (on a plate or tray) and then across a paper. This will make tire tracks on the paper, just like the artwork on the endpapers of the story.

If it's warm enough, you can also let your child play with this concept of printmaking outside with water (or even mud) and construction vehicle toys.

Art: Showing Motion and Speed

Mighty Flatbed brings more supplies to the crew so they can continue their work. There are lines behind the truck that show the motion of the vehicle moving quickly forward. Those blurred lines at the rear of the truck depict both direction and speed. Discuss this with your child (and try to find examples) while looking at the pictures in the story. They may or may not understand this fully, but it will introduce them to the concept of showing motion in their drawings.

Ask your child if they would like to draw a picture that uses lines behind an object to show it moving. This can be done with any art medium: paint, colored pencil, crayons, markers, even paper collage. Get creative and enjoy making some art together.

Social Studies:
Helping Others - Part of a Team

Ask your child what the trucks do when they see the big plans with lots to do, and wonder if it's too much for their little crew? That's right, the cement truck honks his horn and calls for help! "What happens next," you can say to your child? Yes, the other workers hear that the crew needs help. What do they do? They come fast to join the team!

You can discuss together times that your "crew," or family, has a big job to complete, maybe too much for one person to do alone. What about times when there are lots of toys out that need to be put away? Or so many dishes on the table after dinner that need to go back to the kitchen to be cleaned? What about a basketful of clothes, just out of the dryer, that all need to be folded?

Does your child hear the call for help when you ask them to clean up their toys or clear their dishes? It could become a fun game to call out, "Honk! Honk!" (or another sound your family comes up with) when you need their help with a job. This lesson from the story can help your young child understand that they are part of a team (their family) and everyone has a job to do to help complete the big plans for each day!

Math: Counting to 10

All ten trucks appear on the two-page spread where we read, "Rolling, rumbling, revving hard, ten big trucks meet in the yard." Have your child point to each truck and count them. If they are not able to do this on their own, you can touch each and count out loud for them to see and hear.

You can also count how many trucks are on the right page and how many are on the left page. There are five trucks on each! This is introducing your child to the mathematical concept of addition. Counting objects on a page can be done with any story that you read and helps to provide a solid math foundation for your young child.

Science: Sunrise and Sunset

A young child will just be beginning to take notice of a sunrise or sunset. They may not know the difference between these two yet. It's a great time to talk with your child about how a sunrise happens in the morning when the sun rises up in the sky for the day. A sunset occurs at night when the sun sets (kind of like sits), down for the night. After explaining this concept to your child, have them look for the page where the sunrise occurs. (on the title page before the story begins). The sun is rising up behind the buildings. The sunrise continues on the following page when the trucks wake up to the morning light.

Have your child find the page near the end of the story when the sun sets. The sunset is located in a smaller picture on the last page before the moon and starry sky are seen. As the crew leaves for the day, the sun is setting behind the hills.

How do you know if it's sunrise or sunset in an illustration? Without the text, it might be confusing. We read that the trucks are waking to the light when we see the sunrise. In the sunset image, we know that the trucks have been working since morning and are now leaving at the end of the day, so the sun must be setting because it's evening.

Language Arts: Go-Along Books

If your child enjoys reading about trucks or construction work, there are many books you can find to go along with the subject matter. A few favorites are:

• *Digger, Dozer, Dumper* by Hope Vestergaard

- *Supertruck* by Stephen Savage

- *Roadwork Construction Crew* by Sally Sutton

- *Goodnight, Goodnight, Construction Site* by Sherri Duskey Rinker (Written and illustrated by the same author and illustrator as *Mighty, Mighty Construction Site*. This book is a fun bedtime read-aloud.)

Social Studies:
Big or Small - Working Together

Skid is small, fast, and can make tight turns in small spaces. Dozer is big, bulky, and impressive, but even he can't do everything by himself. Ask your child if they think the big bulldozer or the small skid truck can get all the work done without help from the other. No, they can't! The bulldozer can lift heavy things and move them. The small vehicle can't do that. But the small skid can break big rocks to pieces so that the bulldozer can roll through and move them. They have to work together to get all the rocks cleared.

Ask your child if they sometimes need help to get things done. Do they think *you* need help to get jobs done? Discuss how everyone needs help sometimes. It doesn't matter if we're big or small—we can all contribute and help one another!

(This lesson can tie into the Social Studies: Parts of a Team lesson.)

Language Arts: Vocabulary

Learning new words (building vocabulary) is one of the six early literacy skills that will benefit your child's future reading success (see the introduction to *More Before* for the entire list). It's much easier to learn to read a word that you already know. Sounding out a word that you don't know is harder. Having a large vocabulary in place before learning to read will be a benefit to your child.

Reading different kinds of books with your child will introduce them to new sets of words. For instance, this story selection is adding construction words, including specialty work vehicle names and uses, to their vocabulary. When you read your child a book about cooking (like *Bunny Cakes*), then they are learning vocabulary words relating to food, cooking techniques, etc.

Here are a few of the construction vocabulary words found in the story. Feel free to tell your child the meanings of a few of these words if they're interested (some children will be mildly interested while some will be *extremely* so!). There are obviously many, many other construction-related words in the story. You can look online for the meanings of those words if your child wants to know more.

- **crew** - a group of workers who are doing a job together

- **churn** - to move liquid about (kind of like shaking it up)

- **trench** - a narrow ditch

- **hauling** - to use effort to drag something

- **cooperation** - a group working together

- **construction site** - a place where workers are doing jobs to build something

Digger, Dozer, Dumper by Hope Vestergaard has detailed descriptions of the different construction trucks that are found in *Mighty, Mighty Construction Site*. It also has other vehicles that can be found in your community like fire trucks, ambulances, and trash trucks.

Drama and Early Literacy: Acting Out Action Words

The trucks are very active as they work. Below is a list of some of the actions that the vehicles do throughout their day. Take turns acting things out or have your child act out the different words as you say them. This activity will help your child build their vocabulary and make connections between a word and its meaning.

- Stretch

- Drop

- Lift

- Push

- Dig

- Scoop

- Grab

- Honk

- Spin

- Wave

Social Studies: Vehicle Safety - Sounds

About halfway through the story, Loader fills his bucket with dirt and the next line says, "Beep - Beep - Beep! as Loader backs." Ask your child why the truck beeps when it backs up. If they don't know, you could play a game with them where you stand behind them, and while facing away from you, they back up into you. Ask them if they can see what's behind them without looking? Even if we check behind us and then start to back up, a person could still walk into our path if they aren't paying attention. Trucks that work around lots of other vehicles or people are designed to make a sound as they back up to let those around them know

78

they are moving in an unexpected way—backwards. Be on the lookout with your child for trucks beeping as they back up. Head to any construction site or a large home improvement or hardware store to improve your chances of hearing a vehicle equipped with back-up beeping.

This is something you can help your child learn through play. Grab a couple of vehicles and act out the trucks loading up their bucket and then "Beep - Beep - Beep" as it backs up. Physically moving the toys around as they make the sound will help them learn and retain the concept of this safety lesson.

Social Studies: Moving Mountains

Sometimes jobs or things that need to be done seem too big or too hard for us to accomplish. But even huge jobs can be done in tiny pieces or steps. The construction crew trucks move dirt one scoop at a time. The text says, "These pals move MOUNTAINS every day!" Ask your child if they think it's possible to move a mountain. If they say yes, ask them how. If they say no, you can discuss moving a mountain one shovelful at a time. Would that be possible? It might take a long time, but almost anyone could move one shovel's worth of dirt. If you do that enough times, eventually the whole mountain will be moved.

This can be an important lesson for little ones who can become easily overwhelmed by completing daily tasks. Even picking up toys can be something that looks like too much to do. Next time the toys need to be picked up, remind your child to focus on putting one toy away. And then another. And another. Soon the whole room will be clean!

Playtime: Learning Through Play

There are many learning opportunities and details in *Mighty, Mighty Construction Site* that can be acted out in play with your child. Toy vehicles (construction trucks if available, or just cars and trucks) and some painter's tape can turn your floor or table into a construction site! Make pathways or roads and parking spaces. Show your child how a truck would stop at an intersection, pull into a parking space, or drive down a road. Use tape to map out trenches to lay pipe into. Drinking straws could make great pipe sections. You can add blocks or LEGO® to the construction site and move them around with the trucks or make buildings with them.

Imaginative play of real-life situations will help your child make connections between what they see in real life and what they can do. They can't go out and drive a bulldozer at a real construction site, but they can pretend that they are. They see trucks pass by on

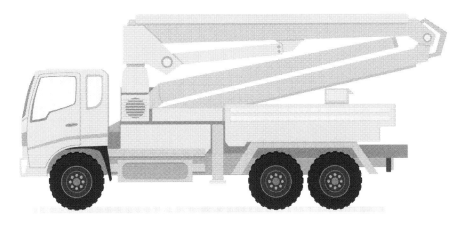

the road transporting supplies, like in the story, and then they can stack up blocks on their toy truck and make-believe that they're taking goods from one place to another.

Pushing and pulling rolling cars and trucks will teach them the beginnings of physics. If they push the truck it will continue rolling for a while before it comes to a stop. When they roll it down a ramp, it goes faster. If they stack lots of blocks on top of a truck, it takes more effort to push it. You don't have to tell or teach them any of this; it's simply how children learn. Hands-on play piques their interest and curiosity, then they test out their thoughts and questions and see what happens. Fred "Mister" Rogers said, "Play is often talked about as if it were a relief from serious learning. But for children, play *is* serious learning. Play is really the work of childhood."

Visual Learning:
Construction Site Videos or Shows

Search online for construction site videos for preschoolers. Preview or be sure to watch with your child if you play a video found online. Bob the Builder is a construction site-themed preschool tevelvision show that encourages problem solving, teamwork, and a positive attitude.

Social Studies:
Recognition of Work Well Done

It's nice to be told, good work, well done, or nice job, when you've worked hard! As the other crew of trucks heads off at the end of the day, "Crane truck waves. 'Great work today!' The crew drives off, engines loud, feeling tired, but strong and proud." Sometimes, having someone notice the hard work you've put into a job and say, "Great work," helps us to feel proud of what we've done. Remember to acknowledge your child when they try to do hard things and to praise them for their efforts and accomplishments. You can also (by modeling and instruction) help your child learn how to recognize others' work and tell them good job, too!

*The story disk for **Mighty, Mighty Construction Site** should be placed by your child near the construction site area on the storybook map.*

OWL BABIES

Title: *Owl Babies*
Author: Martin Waddell
Illustrator: Patrick Benson
Copyright: 1992
(Note: Choose a paperback or hardback copy of this book if you're able; the board book is slightly condensed and does not contain every illustration.)

Summary

Three owl babies wait for their mother to return in the night. They comfort one another and rejoice when their mother eventually swoops back to their nest.

Bible

For Parent:
Psalm 91:4-5, "He will cover you with his feathers, and under his wings you will find refuge; his faithfulness will be your shield and rampart. You will not fear the terror of night…"

After reading the selected story, this verse seems to be the perfect metaphor for the protection we can find in God. The owl babies feared the terror of night, the darkness, and the things that moved in the dark. They were fearful because their mother was not with them. As soon as she returned, they forgot their fear and danced with happiness.

When we pair Psalm 91:4-5 with Isaiah 41:10a (the verse below, for your child) we begin to see the life that God intends for us. God does not want us to live in fear. Isaiah 41:10a says, "So do not fear, for I am with you…" God wants us to be like the baby owls who are fearless when their mother is with them. When we focus on God and declare that he is our refuge, he is with us. We can then live with the confidence of little ones who feel safe simply because their mother or father is with them.

For Child:
Isaiah 41:10a, "So do not fear, for I am with you; do not be dismayed, for I am your God."

For a young child, you can shorten this verse to, "So do not fear, for I am with you." Just like the baby owls who were not afraid when their mother was with them, you can teach your little one that because God is always with us, we do not need to be frightened.

Social Studies: Siblings

Sarah, Percy, and Bill are siblings: one sister and two brothers who live with their owl mother. If your child is an only child, this is a chance to introduce the concept of siblings. If your child has siblings, this story provides an excellent opportunity to discuss the family relationships of brothers and sisters. Who's the oldest or youngest in your child's family? How should brothers and sisters treat each other? How do Sarah, Percy, and Bill treat each other? Are they fighting or being mean to one another? Are they comforting and supporting each other during a scary situation? These discussions are a great time to talk with your child about how you want your family to treat each other.

Teaching Tip:
After you've read the book several times, insert your children's names in place of Sarah, Percy, and Bill, as you read agin. Children love to hear their name in a book, and this is a silly and fun way to personalize the story. If you only have one child, you could insert their name in for one of the owl baby's names.

Science: Where Do Owls Nest?

There are over 200 species of owls, and they live in many different habitats. Different types of owls will nest in hollowed-out trees or cacti, in burrows underground (made by other animals), in bushes, barns, or abandoned nests from other large birds. In the story selection, the three owls and their mother live in "a hole in the trunk of a tree."

Owls do not spend much time or effort building elaborate nests. Instead, they find a ready-made space protected from the elements and predators. The owls' home provides shelter and a place to sleep while the mother gets food for the baby owls. With their basic needs met, the owl babies can focus on growing and learning. You can talk to your child about how children need the same things to be able to grow and learn.

If you're playing the Animal Classification Game, create your own card by drawing or cutting out a picture and gluing it to an index card. Or use the owl card provided in the index to add to your collection.

Science: What Do Owls Eat?

While their mother is gone, Sarah says, "She'll bring us mice and things that are nice." Owls are carnivores, which means that they eat meat. Owls prey on various small animals: mice, rats, rabbits, moles, and amphibians, as well as lizards, insects, and smaller birds. After eating, owls cough up pellets made up of the undigestible parts of their food (hair and bones). You can dissect a pellet and find the bones of their prey and learn what they ate. When your child is older, this is a fascinating science project! For now, talking together and introducing the concept of a carnivore diet is enough.

Art:
Illustrations - Adding Details to the Text

A story can be text only. Before the printing press, this is how most books were written. But many *details* can be added to a story through the illustrations, without adding additional text.

On the first page of the story, we learn through the text that Sarah, Percy, and Bill live with their owl mother in a tree. In the illustration to the right, we see that the three baby owls are of different sizes. This is a simple fact that is not noted in the introductory paragraph. We also see that the owl babies are white and fluffy. The owl babies in their juvenile stage don't look the same as their mature owl mother. These are details that we observe through the image, and these details are automatically added to our understanding of the story.

See if your child notices the owl babies being different sizes. Later in the story, the owls each sit on a separate branch which seems to be based on their size/weight. If your child doesn't notice on their own, you might ask, "Hey, are all the owls the same size?" Or you could say, "What do you notice about the owls in this picture?"

Math: Counting and Pairs

The book's very first image, three owl babies with their mother behind them, provides a fun opportunity for your child to practice counting. Ask your child to look at the owls. How many owls are there? Let's count their beaks. How many feet does each owl have? How many feet are there all together? How many eyes does each owl have?

For an older child, you can introduce the concept of pairs. A pair equals two things. We use the word pair most often when we refer to socks, shoes, mittens, and gloves. You can talk about what parts of our bodies come in pairs. Our eyes, ears, hands, feet, knees, and elbows all come in sets of two. You can expose your child to the concept of skip counting by showing them how you would count the owl's eyes by twos

... 2, 4, 6, 8. This is simply something for them to hear you doing and begin to understand that there are different ways that things can be counted. (This concept is also discussed in the *Toy Boat*, Math: Counting Pairs lesson.)

Language Arts:
Early Literacy - Questions and Exclamations

Some children have a hard time knowing the difference between asking you a question versus telling you something. They might say, "Can I ask you something?" Then proceed to tell you, "It's hot outside."

The story selection offers an excellent opportunity to talk with your child about questions and exclamatory sentences. On the second page, it says:

> "Where's Mommy?" asked Sarah.
> "Oh my goodness!" said Percy.
> "I want my mommy!" said Bill.

This refrain is repeated many times throughout the story and will give your child plenty of opportunities to think about and practice what they learn in this lesson.

After you've read the story several times with your child, read slowly what each owl baby says. Then ask them which owl is asking a question. If they don't know, you can repeat the sentence and exaggerate the word, "*asked* Sarah." Talk with him about how the other two sentences say, "*said* Percy" and "*said* Bill." But Sarah's sentence says "asked."

You can also point to the question mark after "Where's Mommy?" Trace the shape with your finger and explain that this character (symbol) tells us that Sarah is asking a question. Then show your child the exclamation points after Percy and Bill's sentences. Again, trace the line down and the dot underneath and tell them how this symbol is used to show the reader that the character is making an exclamation.

This activity touches on two of the six early literacy skills (see the introduction to *More Before* for the entire list). **Letter knowledge** and **print awareness** are both highlighted by looking closely at the question mark and exclamation point character shapes and meanings with your child.

Language Arts:
Early Literacy - Narrative Skills

Narrative skills is another important early literacy skill. When your child can sequence events and retell stories, it shows that they are comprehending what they are reading or hearing. There are several things you can do to encourage this skill. Ask open-ended questions about the story or have them name feelings of characters in the story. Have your child make predictions about what is going to happen in the story or come up with a different ending.

Here are some sample questions to help you apply these early literacy skill builders to the story selection. How do you think the baby owls felt when they woke up and their mother was gone? How do they feel when she returns? Do you think their mother will come back? Why did the owl mother leave? What do you think the mother is doing while she's gone? What's a different way the story could end? Make up your own questions too, and apply these types of questions to any book you read with your child to continue building their narrative skills!

Art: Viewpoint

When the owl babies wake up in the night and realize their owl mother is gone, the viewpoint from the previous page has changed. Suddenly the reader is seeing the baby owls from high up above. We are looking down at them, and they look small on the floor of their home in the tree. Like the viewpoint lesson in *Bunny Cakes* when Max seems small, perhaps the illustrator of *Owl Babies* chose to change the viewpoint purposefully to make the baby owls appear little.

There are several different changes in viewpoint throughout the story that you can point out or discuss with your child. Later in the story, on the page that begins, "It was dark in the woods", the viewpoint changes again. Now it is as if the reader is down low in the woods looking way up at the owls waiting for their mother. The babies look very tiny, and the woods appear immense!

When the mother owl comes back, near the end of the story, again, it is as though we are up high. We see the mother owl as if we were above her, and way down below her are the baby owls waiting on a branch. This viewpoint shows both the vastness of the woods and how small the baby owls are, in relation to the mother owl, trees and woods.

You can share this illustration technique with your child through informal discussion. You might ask them on different pages if the baby owls look big or small? Does the forest seem large? Is the tree that the owls live in tall? These simple questions will allow them to process and think about how the same object can look different (bigger or smaller) at times. They don't need to know *why* yet. It's enough for them just to begin noticing these changes.

Art: Nighttime Illustrations

The night sky illustrations that appear throughout the story selection are a beautiful bright blue. This contrast to the dark, almost black, depictions of the woods is a vivid surprise when you turn the page and see the blue background with twinkling white stars. Sometimes it's a small area of sky around the edges of their hole in the tree, while other times the page is filled with the starlit backdrop.

Let your child try their hand at creating a night sky picture. Give your child dark blue construction paper and white paint, crayons, oil pastels or a white marker to make the stars. They can add green leaves or some baby owls too! (There is a similar activity in the Art: Night Sky lesson for *Waiting Is Not Easy!*)

Language Arts: Repetition

Repetition in children's books is a literary device that an author chooses to use to emphasize a point, create a rhythm, or link ideas together. Repetition helps children make connections more quickly and is a bit like "memory Velcro®"... it helps things stick in a child's brain!

Sarah and Percy say different things throughout the story. Bill, however, simply repeats, "I want my mommy!" This repetition likely emphasizes the point that all the owl babies really want their owl mother to come back. While Sarah and Percy are trying to be brave or practical in their comments, they all want their mommy to come back!

Social Studies: Being Brave

The owl babies had a chance to be brave! Alone in the dark, waiting for their mother, they naturally felt afraid. Talk with your child about times they feel scared and how they have a chance, each time they get that feeling, to be brave. Being brave doesn't mean that you don't feel afraid, but that you try your best not to let that feeling stop you from doing what you need to do. Ask your child if they think you can be scared and be brave at the same time? Do they believe the owl babies were scared but choosing to be brave even though they were afraid? What did they do that helped them to be brave?

"'I think we should *all* sit on *my* branch,' said Sarah. And they did, all three together." By sitting together, the owl babies were able to draw comfort and strength from each other to help them while they waited for their mother. Remind your child that asking for help from a friend or parent when you're scared is a great way to gain the support you might need to be brave. Sometimes we have to do things alone, too, and that is a perfect time to remember that God is always with us!

Social Studies: Stay Calm Thinking

While Bill is voicing the thought that all the owl babies have, "I want my mommy!", Sarah and Percy are practicing their *stay calm* thinking, or for an older child, you could call it crisis thinking. Where might their mother have gone? Instead of rushing to thoughts that she'd left them alone forever, they start with what she is likely be doing. She's gone hunting—yes, to get us food, they say to each other. She'll be back soon, they remind themselves. Thinking about the truth in a scary situation can help us keep calm and remember what else we should do.

Having a plan and talking with your child about what to do if they get lost or need help is always a good idea. Remind your child as you read the story selection that Sarah and Percy are using *stay calm* thinking.

*Find the tree with the hole in it on the storybook map; place the **Owl Babies** story disk on the tree.*

RED KNIT CAP GIRL AND THE READING TREE

Title: *Red Knit Cap Girl and the Reading Tree*

Author: Naoko Stoop

Illustrator: Naoko Stoop

Copyright: 2014

Summary

After finding a hollow tree in the woods, Red Knit Cap Girl and her woodland friends work together, finding something unique they each can contribute to make a special place they will all enjoy!

Parent Information: Your child might notice or comment that the girl is wearing a hat, a scarf, and boots even though it is "too hot to run and play." *Red Knit Cap Girl and the Reading Tree* is one book in a series beginning with *Red Knit Cap Girl*. It's likely that the author chose not to change Red Knit Cap Girl's attire to fit the weather at the beginning of the story because her clothing is what *defines* her character.

Bible

For Parent:

1 Corinthians 12:26, "If one member suffers, all suffer together; if one member is honored, all rejoice together."

In Paul's first letter to the Corinthians, he writes about the body of Christ (all Christians) working together as one body. Each person is a part of something greater than himself, and without each member, the body would be weaker. Our story is a lovely picture of a group working together, each contributing what they can, to make something that none of them could have created alone. Like Red Knit Cap Girl and her

woodland friends, we as Christians can have a significant impact for Christ when we work together, each contributing his or her unique talents. At the end of the story, the group enjoys the fruits of their labor and "all rejoice together."

For Child:
Numbers 10:32b, "...we will share with you whatever good things the Lord gives us."

In this verse, Moses is asking Hobab to accompany the Israelites along their journey during their exodus from Egypt. Moses appeals to Hobab (in Numbers 10:31) saying, "Please do not leave us. You know where we should camp in the wilderness, and you can be our eyes. If you come with us, we will share with you whatever good things the Lord gives us."

Red Knit Cap Girl and the Reading Tree contains many examples of friends sharing the good things they've been blessed with. Discuss with your child the benefits of sharing. Ask them for examples of how they can share with others.

Science: Weather - Outdoor Activities

The beginning of our story, says, "it was too hot to run and too hot to play." Ask your child if there are times when it is too hot to run or play outside? What do they like to do instead? Do they play inside? Or read? Maybe they play in a sprinkler to cool down or go swimming. Sometimes it's too cold to play outside or too rainy.

At times, the weather and temperature can make it less pleasant to play outdoors, just like it did for Red Knit Cap Girl. Ask your child what she did instead? That's right! She found a shady spot and read a book. She was still outside. What made reading a book in a shady spot more comfortable than running and playing? They might notice that she was sitting still so she wasn't getting as hot or sweaty as she would have if she was running around. Or that being in the shade is cooler than being in the sun. If they don't think of these things on their own, you can ask them if they get hot when they run around. Or ask them if sitting in the shade is more comfortable than sitting in the hot sun?

Art: Book Illustrations

After reading the story at least once, see if your child takes notice of the background of the pictures on each page. The illustrations for this story were created with acrylic paint, ink, and pencil. These are basic art supplies used in illustrating. The fascinating part of the Red Knit Cap Girl's illustrations is the background that the drawing and paint were applied to. The pictures were painted and drawn directly onto plywood.

Your child is likely not yet familiar enough with woodgrain to recognize it on the pages of the story. Look around your house for woodgrain on furniture items or flooring that you can examine together.

This also provides an excellent opportunity to go on a scavenger hunt to a local hardware store and find plywood to look at in person. Take the book with you so that you can show your child the pages next to the woodgrain on a piece of plywood. You could even buy some plywood for your child to paint on and experiment with at home. If you choose to bring home plywood to paint on, you will also need a pen with black ink (Sharpie brand would work well), a pencil, acrylic paints, and brushes.

Art: Paper is Made From Wood (Trees)

Paper, on which you would normally see a book's illustrations painted or drawn, is made using wood from trees. Isn't it interesting that the illustrator chose to use wood in a more natural form as the background for her illustrations? Naoko Stoop's choice to illustrate this story directly onto wood seems to makes subtle connections between trees, paper, and reading.

Ask your child if they know how paper is made? What does it come from? Trees! Paper is made by taking raw wood from trees and turning it into pulp. The pulp is like a thin soup made from wood fibers, water, and chemicals used to turn the raw wood into pulp and then into paper.

Once it's soupy enough, the pulp mixture is sprayed onto screens, creating a mat. That mat then has the water removed and is dried out. After drying, the mat is run through hot rollers to squeeze out any remaining water, dry it out completely, and compress (flatten) it into a continuous roll of paper.

You can search online for papermaking videos. There are animated ones and videos of real factories readily available for you and your child to watch together and see how the papermaking process works!

Science: Animals

If you're playing the Animal Classification Game, this story selection provides many animals to add to your cards. Below is a list of all the woodland animals we meet in this book. Additional science lessons will introduce two animals, beaver and hedgehog, to your child and help them learn more about these interesting animals. Create your own cards by drawing or cutting out a picture and gluing it to an index card. Or use the cards provided in the back of the manual.

squirrel
rabbit (white bunny)
bear
hedgehog
beaver

fox

deer

duck

turtle

sheep

Science: Animals - Beaver

Beavers are large rodents, mostly nocturnal (awake and active at night), and semiaquatic (they spend a large portion of their time in the water as a regular part of their routine).

Rodents make up a group of animals including rats, mice, squirrels, hamsters, porcupines, and more. They have large front teeth on both the top and bottom jaw that grow continuously and are used to gnaw wood, get into food (nuts, seeds, etc.), and bite predators.

Beavers have webbed feet and a large, oval-shaped flat tail that helps them swim. They cut down trees with their front teeth and use the trees to build dams and to create ponds and lodges. A lodge is a beaver's home. It is a small dome-shaped house made of woven grass and sticks and coated in mud. (Your child may remember that in *Go to Sleep, Little Farm*, the girl imitates the beaver weaving "a bed in a bog," or building its lodge.)

Show your child a photo online of a beaver lodge with an underwater entrance. You can also search for a picture of a tree that has been felled by a beaver. What's left of the trunk has a distinct sharpened point that is different from a tree cut by an ax or saw. There are also photos of trees that are in the process of being felled by a beaver. These trees show an hourglass shape in the area that has been gnawed.

If you're playing the Animal Classification Game, create your own card by drawing or cutting out a picture and gluing it to an index card. Or use the beaver card provided in the index to add to your collection.

Science: Animals - Hedgehog

Hedgehogs are not native to the Americas; they are found through parts of Europe, Asia, and Africa, and in New Zealand. A hedgehog is a spiny mammal. Its spines (stiff hollow hairs) are not poisonous or barbed, and do not easily come off of their body. They look similar to a porcupine but are not related. Most hedgehogs are nocturnal (active at night), and all of them can hibernate. Some hedgehogs are active in the day, and some choose not to hibernate.

Hedgehogs have a unique way of defending themselves. They can roll into a tight ball, which makes their spines all point outwards. This protects their face, feet, and belly, which do not have spines. Search online for pictures of a hedgehog rolled up and show your child what it looks like. It's like a spiky ball!

There are many children's picture books featuring hedgehogs. A quick online search of your library should provide possible titles to choose from if your child would like to read educational books to learn more about hedgehogs, or stories that include hedgehogs as characters. One option to consider is Beatrix Potter's *The Tale of Mrs. Tiggy-Winkle*. This is a classic story with an English hedgehog as the main character.

If you're playing the Animal Classification Game, create your own card by drawing or cutting out a picture and gluing it to an index card. Or use the hedgehog card provided in the index to add to your collection.

Science: Seasons

Our story starts when it's too hot to enjoy playing outside. In the beginning, the illustrations show the trees with green leaves, green grass, and blooming flowers. As we near the end of the book, the colors have changed. The trees and grass are a mixture of fall colors: red, orange, yellow, and brown. We read that, "They read every day until the air turns clear and crisp and cold. It is autumn now..." On the next page with Owl and Moon, it says, "All summer, all fall ..."

Now is a great time to show your child the pictures and talk about seasons! This story follows the characters from summer through fall. In areas of the world that have all four seasons, summer and fall would be followed by winter and then spring.

Ask your child to help you make a list of things that happen during each season. If they are entirely unfamiliar with seasons, looking at pictures online of different seasons, or getting a book about the seasons from the library and reading it together might give them more ideas to add to their list.

Math: Basic Counting and Story Problem Foundations

The pages where Deer, Duck, and Turtle bring their books to the nook provide some great opportunities to work on counting. Ask your child how many books does Deer have? How many books does Duck have? How many books does Turtle have? How many turtles are there?

Questions for your older child might include how many animals are there all together? If mama turtle gave the blue book to one baby, and the green book to one baby, and kept the red book, how many books would each turtle be carrying? If mama turtle gave the blue book to one baby, and the green book to one baby, how many books would mama turtle have left? These questions are the foundation of story problem math skills that your child will develop further in elementary school. Hearing math questions worded in these ways and with visual representations (in the illustrations) that they can look at or point to as they count or figure out the problem, will give them an advantage when they encounter word problems in a math book later on!

92

Language Arts: Folklore, Fables, and Sly Fox

While the other animals in our story are simply called Bear, White Bunny, Deer, or Hedgehog, you or your child might have noticed that the fox is named Sly Fox. This portrayal of the fox as cunning or the villain in children's literature has roots in both myth and folklore. Aesop, an early Greek storyteller who wrote what are now known as Aesop's Fables, characterized foxes as tricksters. This depiction, along with similar portrayals from other writers, has stuck, and continues to occur in current children's stories. If you or your child is interested, you could check out Aesop's Fables from the library (or search online) and read "The Fox and the Grapes" or "The Fox and the Crow."

Thankfully, in our story, Sly Fox learns the *value* of sharing books and returns the book she's taken so that everyone can enjoy it!

Language Arts: Reading - Book Choices

Sometimes we read books for school or work that we don't get to pick out for ourselves. Most of the time, though, we choose books that relate to something we are interested in or enjoy. See if your child notices what kind of book White Bunny is reading. If they don't notice or point out the carrot on bunny's book, you might ask them what type of book White Bunny has. Why would a bunny read about carrots? Because bunnies like to eat vegetables that grow in gardens!

Ask your child what their interests are and make a special trip to the library to pick out books relating to those topics. This practice of finding enjoyable subject matter for each individual to read encourages early literacy, as well as instilling a lifelong love of reading!

Language Arts: Library

A library is a space that holds a collection of books and periodicals for people to borrow and read. Today's libraries often also have music, audiobooks, and movies to borrow and listen to or watch. A library is a wondrous place to let children explore the exciting world of books! It's necessary to help your child understand the rules or expectations that are important to follow at a library. Explain that lots of people use the library, and many of them like to sit and read or work in the calm space that the library provides. It's considerate to help keep that space quiet.

Next time you take your little one to the library, try the whisper game! When you arrive at the library, remind your child that they can help keep the library space quiet for everyone and that you want to play a game with them. It's called the whisper game, and the only rule is that you have to whisper the whole time you're inside the library.

The exception to the quiet library space rule is if you attend a children's story time or other child-focused activity at the library. These programs often encourage children to participate during singing, finger plays, counting, and reading aloud. This is a time that kids do not need to be quiet.

Language Arts: Vocabulary

In our story, Bear asks, "What is it for?" when they look at the nook that squirrel has found. Nook is likely a new word for your child. While Red Knit Cap Girl has an idea, and ends up using the space to create a library, the story doesn't explain the actual meaning of the word nook.

Nook is defined as a corner or recess (an area further back from the rest), particularly one that offers protection or security.

In the story, the nook makes a great library because it does provide protection; it keeps their books "safe and dry." Take your child on a search around your house for any areas that might be used as a reading nook. A couple of places to look might be under sturdy tables or in corners behind chairs. A blanket fort can make a cozy nook if you can't find a comfortable or safe place to use within your home. If the weather is pleasant, a search outdoors can also provide appropriate spaces to tuck away in. Have your child snuggle in with a blanket and a book for relaxed reading time in their newfound nook!

Language Arts: Newspaper

The birds in our story don't have a book to share. Instead, they bring a newspaper. Like books, newspapers are made up of written words that form stories and articles from which we can learn. Newspapers are a "periodical," in that they are distributed daily, weekly, or at regular intervals, and they typically cover events that are currently taking place.

Some children today have never seen a newspaper. If your child isn't familiar with a newspaper, buy one at a gas station to look at together so they can understand and become familiar with it. Be sure to preview and provide a section that is child-friendly and appropriate.

Early Learning and Literacy: Getting Ideas from Reading

Beaver wants to share something too but doesn't have a book. Then he gets an idea! Look with your child at the illustration of Beaver and Red Knit Cap Girl sitting on the log reading the newspaper. Ask your child, "Where did Beaver get his idea to build a bookshelf? Yes, that's right,

94

he got it from reading the article in the newspaper!" (If you've already read *Bunny Cakes* together, remind your child how Max got his idea to draw the Red Hot-Marshmallow Squirters!)

Ask your child how they learn about new things. Their answers might include: from shows, watching mom, dad, or an older sibling do something, asking questions, or reading about something in a book.

Explain to your child that reading books, magazines, or newspapers, as well as looking thing up online are some ways that all of us (even mom, dad, and other adults) learn new things! Our world is so vast and amazing that we will never run out of things to learn about. Knowing how to find answers to questions that we have is an important life skill, and it's never too early to start a dialogue with your children about how to find answers to their questions and learn new things!

Social Studies: Ways You Can Help Others

While many of the animals have books to share and help create the library, some of them do not. Beaver doesn't have a book to share but gets an idea of something that he can do to contribute. He can gnaw wood and create a bookshelf. The sheep may or may not have added books, but as the weather gets colder, they bring what they have to share ... which is warm wool blankets! Owl and Moon work together to offer something as well. Moon shines her light down during the night so that Owl can see to write. They make a sign that says "Library." Share these examples with your child.

A great way to explore this idea further with your child is to discuss your family. How does each member of the group/family contribute to help one an-other? Let your child dictate a list of things that each person in the family does and write down their list.

For example, parents' roles might include: working to make money, taking care of the children, cleaning the house, making meals, fixing broken things, etc. Older siblings might do laundry, clean their own room, and play with younger kids. What ways can a younger child help? They can pick up their toys, clear their dishes from the table, help get things from other rooms for Dad and Mom, draw a picture to cheer someone up, or have a positive attitude.

Social Studies: Gratitude - Being Thankful

After all the characters have worked together to make the library, they enjoy an evening of reading. The "little ones who can't read yet" thank Red Knit Cap Girl for reading aloud to them so that they can enjoy the stories! Red Knit Cap Girl thanks each one of her friends who helped make the library. It's good to be thankful for the things that other people do to help you and to show your gratitude by saying thank you.

Ask your child if they enjoy hearing books read aloud to them. To encourage gratitude and model that behavior for them, you could thank them for sitting still and listening when you're reading to them. Or thank them for picking up their toys, clearing their dishes from the table, or being kind to their siblings.

*Let your child place the story disk for **Red Knit Cap Girl and the Reading Tree** at the Library tree on the storybook map.*

THANKS FOR THANKSGIVING

Title: *Thanks for Thanksgiving*

Author: Julie Markes

Illustrator: Doris Barrette

Copyright: 2004

Summary

A lyrical list, with whimsical illustrations, of big and small things in our lives that are worth being thankful for, ending with the most important ... family.

Bible

For Parent:

Philippians 4:6, "Do not be anxious about anything, but in every situation, by prayer and petition, with thanksgiving, present your requests to God."

Not being anxious is easier or harder for different people. When we have children, it may get harder not to be worried. We want the best for our kids, and we spend our days and nights doing what we can to keep them safe and happy. But God loves our kids even more than we do. He is clear in Philippians 4:6 that we are not to be anxious, but to come to him with our requests and also with thanksgiving!

Why do you think God asks us to come to him with thanksgiving when we're presenting our requests to him? He knows that gratitude strengthens our hearts and allows our minds to focus on the truth, that God is with us and for us, even during the hard times.

96

For Child:

1 Chronicles 16:34a, "Give thanks to the Lord, for he is good..."

With repetition, even young children can remember God's word. This verse is short and would make a fun start/finish game to play with your child. After reading it and saying it to your child several times, you would say, "Give thanks to the Lord..." and then have them say, "for he is good!" You can then trade and have them start with "Give thanks to the Lord..." and you finish with, "for he is good!" Hiding God's word in our hearts is a great way to remember truths about God. Playing a memorization game with them in this way will allow them to remember an important truth: God is good! It will also teach them to give thanks to God.

Cultivating and helping your child learn to be thankful is so important and such a special opportunity you have as their parent. Gratitude increases our sense of well being and makes us happier. It helps us to have a positive mindset, even when some things in our lives are challenging.

Thanksgiving is a time of year when we often focus on gratitude; let's try to make it a part of our daily routine, for ourselves and our children!

Here are some ways to cultivate and include gratitude in daily life:

- Mention something you're grateful for at breakfast each day and ask your child what they're thankful for.

- Thank God for the things he's blessed you with during bedtime prayers.

- Keep a written list where you can see it and have family members add items to it daily.

Remember as you reread your list together now and then to talk about how these blessings are from God.

- When facing a challenge or disappointment, try to think of three things you're thankful for (it can help put things in perspective).

Thanksgiving: Traditions, Turkey, and Pie

Thanksgiving has become a day set aside to spend with family and friends. Many people have turkey and pumpkin pie as part of their feast. Remembering all we've been blessed with and giving thanks is another focus on Thanksgiving.

What makes Thanksgiving special for your family? Talk together with your child about who you spend your time with on this holiday. Family, friends, feeding the homeless, etc.

What are the things that you like to do together that make the day unique? Maybe it's baking pies together the night before, making cranberry orange bread with Grandma for breakfast, watching the parade on TV, going on a brisk walk after the big meal, or playing catch with the football. If your family doesn't do much besides dinner, talk about what special things you could try together to create memories and enjoy your time together.

Where do you spend the holiday? Do you travel to be with family or friends on Thanksgiving? Does everyone come to your house?

Thinking through and talking about what your family does on Thanksgiving allows your child to make valuable connections between their understanding of a day/event/holiday, with what it means to your family specifically.

Author's Note: When my oldest daughter was three years old we started a special tradition. I would go alone and secretly pick out a mylar balloon with of one of her favorite cartoon characters on it (sometimes the balloon was several feet tall) and bring it home the night before Thanksgiving. The next morning as we watched the Macy's Thanksgiving Day Parade together on TV (because that was a tradition that I loved from my childhood) I would bring out the balloon as a surprise and let her march around the house as "part of the parade." Often, the character on her balloon would match the character of one of the actual balloons in the parade. We would pause the TV and take a picture of her with her balloon next to the TV screen and the matching/similar parade balloon.

Science: Autumn - Deciduous Trees

Deciduous trees are ones that shed their leaves (their leaves fall off) seasonally. Usually, this happens in autumn. The leaves turn red, orange, and yellow (or "gold" as they did in our story), before falling off, "floating by," or drifting down.

Discuss with your child how trees are different. What kinds of things have they noticed about some trees that are different from other trees? Unlike deciduous trees, evergreen trees, as their name suggests, stay green all year. Christmas trees are evergreens.

Take your child on a nature walk to look at the different trees around your house, your block, or a nearby park. Your child can collect leaves or

pine needles from the trees as you walk and you can help them find out what kinds of trees they came from by doing an internet search for beginner tree identification. (A small field guide to trees specific to your state or region is also great to have on hand.) Collecting leaves can be done any time of year, but is especially fun in fall, when the leaves are turning beautiful colors!

You can use the collected leaves for easy art projects by letting your child trace the shapes, paint over the leaf on a paper and lift for a relief print, or pressing the leaf down evenly onto clay or playdough, leaving an imprint.

Teaching Tip:
Laminating leaves will seal out the oxygen/air and allow the leaves to retain their color. This is a great way to collect fall leaves and create a lasting piece of artwork or booklet displaying all the beautiful fall colors.

Science: Our Brains - Learning

Your child may be excited to do their own "school," or they might be enjoying their playtime. Like the children in this story, they might love running, jumping, swinging, dancing, art, and snuggling up with Mom (or Dad) to read books. All of these options are excellent learning opportunities for your child.

One fantastic thing about our brains is the amount of learning that is happening from the moment we're born (or even before). Conception to age three encompasses a fast and furious time of brain development and learning, all happening through fundamental life experiences, not specialized teaching or instruction.

Albert Einstein said, "Play is the highest form of research." If you feel pressure to begin school with your child, remember that their learning can be based solidly on playing, reading together, and discovering the world around them naturally, and with you by their side. The more formal lessons of learning letters, how to write, worksheets, and phonics can wait. Future lessons will benefit from the connections they're making and the strength they're building through play!

It is crucial to recognize that screens (TVs, movies, tablets, iPads/iPods, smartphones, computers, etc.) have invaded much of children's free time, which is taking time away from their outdoor exploration and physical play. There can certainly be a time and place for including screen time in your child's day, but moderation, and balancing it with outdoor or physical play, is always a good idea.

The information in this lesson isn't something you need to discuss with your child; it is an encouragement to *you* that during these early years of life, learning is happening all the time for your child, especially during and through play.

Science: Wind

If your child doesn't notice or comment on their own, after reading through the story, you can show them the open windows in the classroom illustration. You might ask them if it's sunny or cloudy outside the window? Is it windy or still? How can we tell?

Maybe they noticed the little girl's hair blowing as the wind comes in the window, or the feather and parachute floating through the room. The boat the girl is holding has a sail and flag attached to it that are filled and flapping in the breeze. The window shades aren't lying flat but are blown up towards the ceiling. These are all things you can mention or ask your child about while reading together.

Discuss with your child that wind is just air moving. Light objects like feathers and hair move easily when air passes by, while more substantial objects like people, books, and furniture are unmoved by a normal breeze. Find some light and heavier objects from around the house and have your child try to blow them across a tabletop. This experiment is an example of something moving because of the wind (air moving), being blown from their mouth.

As you run errands or go for walks with your child this week, have them help you look for ways that wind is moving things around them. Leaves on trees, flags, curtains, people's hair, or anything else that they see. Enjoy watching their excitement as they notice all the ways the wind affects things around us!

Art: Music, Dancing, and Fine Art

Things of beauty in our lives often come in the form of music, dancing, and art. What lovely things to be thankful for and to introduce to your young child. Look at the illustration with your child of the boy playing the violin, the girl dancing in her tutu and the little one drawing pictures. Does one of these activities look particularly fun to them?

Your child is likely too young to start playing an instrument yet, but playing different types of music for small children to listen to is a great way to introduce them to the sounds of instruments and the beauty of this art form. Also, giving them rhythm shakers, drumming on pots with a wooden spoon, or turning other household objects into instruments can be a fun way to play along with music and be a basic introduction to keeping a rhythm.

Search online for classic ballet performances (like Swan Lake, the Nutcracker, and others). Share a few minutes of them with your child to introduce them to the graceful art of dance.

Of course, they don't have to take ballet classes to dance. Dancing to any type of music is a good way to exercise, release energy, reduce stress,

100

and build muscle. Dance is an activity that takes athleticism, physical strength, and rhythm. Many dance studios are now offering classes of all kinds for girls and boys. Break out your favorite dancing music and make some memories with your child. A family dance party will put a smile on your child's face, and probably yours too!

Coloring and painting are easy ways to express ourselves artistically, at any age. Babies to grandparents can put crayon, brush, or pencil to paper and create something from nothing. Provide your child with different tools for them to experiment with creatively: paper, crayons, colored pencils, markers, finger paint, watercolor, torn paper, and glue sticks. Magazines with images to tear or cut out are fun, or any other favorite art supplies.

Learning colors and different art terms will come with time. For now, sit down with your child and show them how to make art. Teach by example as you work on a personal piece of artwork. Allow them open time, space, and supplies to create for themselves.

Teaching Tip:
Framing a young child's artwork or designating a section of wall space as a rotating "children's art museum" is a lovely way of encouraging their creativity and adding personalized beauty to your home.

The Importance of Outdoor Play

The story selection includes a list of enjoyable outdoor play activities that are worthy of giving thanks for! Swings, slides, and other playground equipment are a favorite of children around the world and provide a perfect opportunity for children to challenge themselves mentally and physically.

Allowing limited risk in a child's world gives them a chance to build resilience. When a young child tries a challenging obstacle on the playground, they might first need to hold your hand. Most children will learn through that experience that they are stronger than they felt, and next time maybe they only hold your finger ... and after that, they face it alone! This example is a perfect scenario of feeling a level of fear or stress, working through that uncomfortable feeling with help, and then realizing that it's okay to feel scared—you can still push through those feelings and accomplish your goal. (Allowing limited risk is also discussed in the Health: Climbing Trees - Appropriate Risk-Taking for Developmental Growth lesson found in *All the World*.)

Resilience is a critical life skill that you can begin to help your young children build within themselves. Provide opportunities, bring in risk, and allow them to try without fear of failing. Offer your child help when asked, and hold yourself back at times when you want to rush in and save them (unless they're in real danger, in which case, please rush in and save them). Always encourage them and let them use their bravery and learned resilience to continue growing and developing! (Resilience was also discussed in the Character Development: Nurturing Resilience lesson found in *All the World*.)

Outdoor games like hopscotch, jump rope, hide-and-seek, four square, and so many others all provide chances for your child to grow physically and socially. Playing with others, taking turns, and working out disagreements will give your child natural opportunities to practice their social and problem-solving skills.

Benefits of Dress-Up Play for Children

Dress-up is a favorite activity of children and is an excellent opportunity for your child to role play or act out things that aren't a regular part of their lives. It helps them learn more about themselves, their likes, and dislikes by experimenting with new ideas and behaviors safely (while acting like someone else).

Playing dress-up fosters imagination! The possibilities are endless on *who*, *what*, *when*, and *where* they're playing.

It's brain-building too. Acting out can help children internalize and learn things they've heard or seen as they add these things into their play and "experience" them. If you've taken your child to the library a few times, they might play librarian or story time at home. If you read them a book about hot air balloons, don't be surprised when your laundry basket is missing and has become a balloon basket!

Dress-up also allows for emotional development. Despite our best efforts to protect our children and shelter them from scary things in life, they will encounter frightening situations. A sibling falls and breaks an arm, we drive past a car wreck and they see the crushed car with an ambulance nearby, something scary flashes by on TV, etc.—all of these experiences can frighten a child and make them feel helpless.

Children can process these fears through play. They might act out being the doctor and putting the cast on or taking it off a dozen times, or they'll pretend to be the firefighter or paramedic that comes to help the people hurt in the car crash. Re-playing the event and pretending to be one of the adults (people that are helping or in control) is how they are addressing those feelings of fear and helplessness.

Therapy for children, provided by professional therapists, is often in the form of play. If your child has faced trauma or has a need for therapy, seeking a professional is always a good idea. If, however, they are facing smaller, everyday fears, then you are giving them a chance to process their emotions by providing them with role-playing opportunities (dress-up, doll house, cars, etc.).

Do you want to encourage empathy in your child? Play dress-up! By dressing up as others and "living" their life through play, your child has to put themselves in someone else's shoes (literally and figuratively). This activity helps them to think about what others are feeling. The ability to think of others and understand what they might be feeling will help them throughout their lives with all types of relationships.

Dress-up play pushes a child's communication and vocabulary as they think of how a chef, nurse, astronaut, or cowboy might talk. Using words and phrases they wouldn't typically use builds their verbal and thinking skills.

When deciding who gets to be the waiter and customer at the restaurant, the doctor and the patient, or which outfit or props to use with their character, they are problem-solving. What a fun way for your child to practice these essential life skills!

Science: Moon and Stars

Ask your child if they are thankful for the moon and stars? Begin pointing out the moon at different times in the month to your child and discuss how it changes. Sometimes it's just a sliver or crescent, while other times it's like a round ball, full and bright! (Additional lessons and discussions about the moon and stars can be found in *Waiting Is Not Easy!* and *In a Blue Room*.)

Here's a favorite childhood poem about the moon and how it changes by Vachel Lindsay. Share it with your child and be sure to act it out (biting the cookie and kneading the clouds).

The Moon's the North Wind's cooky.
He bites it, day by day,

Until there's but a rim of scraps
That crumble all away.

The South Wind is a baker.
He kneads clouds in his den,
And bakes a crisp new moon that ... greedy
North ... Wind ... eats ... again!

Family

Talk with your child about the family in this story. How many kids are there? Throughout the pages, we see the mom, dad, and three kids. How does that compare to your family? You can talk about being an older or younger brother or sister and what that means to your family. Does your child help set an example for younger siblings and play with them? Or do they get to look up to a big brother or sister and learn from them? In the piggyback ride image, the big brother is sweetly giving his younger sibling a ride. If they're an only child, then they get to have special times and lots of chances to help Mom and Dad each day!

Ask your child what things they can do to be helpful to others in the family. Maybe it's helping you fold laundry or picking up their toys, or helping to entertain a younger sibling or set the table. Including your child in the daily work of family life gives them a sense of purpose and value. Working together is part of what makes a family so extraordinary and helps to build your child's sense of belonging!

The children in Thanks for Thanksgiving loved to play at the park, so have your child place the story disk on the park near the slide and swings.

104

Title: *Toot & Puddle*
Author: Holly Hobbie
Illustrator: Holly Hobbie
Copyright: 1997

Summary

A year in the life of two friends with different personalities and interests, who have adventures at home and away. This sweet story of friendship shows us that being different is okay and being yourself is great!

Bible

For Parent:
Psalm 16: 6, 11, "Lord, you alone are my portion and my cup; you make my lot secure. The boundary lines have fallen for me in pleasant places … You make known to me the path of life; you will fill me with joy in your presence, with eternal pleasures at your right hand."

Toot and Puddle are very different in their personalities, desires, and things they find life-giving and pleasurable. Verse 6 says that the Lord makes our lot secure and that "the boundary lines have fallen for me in pleasant places." Both characters seem to agree that they have a safe and pleasant home. But while Puddle finds it perfect and never wants to leave, Toot loves to travel and see the world.

Allowing God alone to be your portion and cup is not an easy task. So many things vie for our attention, our heart, and our mind each day. Practice looking to God daily and listening for his voice. While Bible study and daily devotional time are important and strengthen our under-

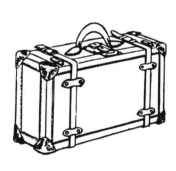

standing of God, don't forget to take advantage of the many small opportunities to pause and ask for help, listen, or simply breathe. These flowing moments are what make up our life. Bringing God into these small routine breaths is one way we can mindfully practice making him alone our portion.

Verse 11 says, "You make known to me the path of life." Wow, we have a God that knows we each have different things that will be fulfilling and life-giving. Not only is that okay, but he will make them known to us! If you struggle with finding which activities, relationships, or causes are pleasurable to you and bring you joy, don't hesitate to ask God to make them known to you. His desire is for us to allow him to be our portion and our cup so that he can fill us with joy!

For Child:
Psalm 19:105, "Your word is a lamp to my feet and a light to my path."

God's word helps us to see the path before us. It keeps us from stumbling or tripping on those things in our way. At night, or in a room you can make very dark, create a curvy path on the floor out of painters tape, post-it notes, a ribbon, whatever you have available. Ask your child to follow or walk on the path while the lights are on.

Now have them turn around and ask them to follow the line back, but this time, in the dark. Is that harder? What if we have obstacles in our way? Is it even harder? Now give them a flashlight and explain that when they turn it on and use it to shine a light on the path, it helps them see where they should walk. God's word (the Bible) is like a lamp to our feet, and it helps us know the direction we should be going and avoid the things in our way.

Science: DNA and Personality

You've probably heard of introverts and extroverts. If not, you've now seen them in action within our story. Puddle is happy and able to recharge while being alone. He enjoys his friends and isn't shy or reclusive, but is comfortable and fulfilled while doing things on his own. This lifestyle is how an introvert thrives.

Toot loves his friend and his home but needs more adventure and interaction to be happy. He wants to see the world and meet new people, and then come home to rest after being filled up and recharged through his travels. Toot is an excellent example of an extrovert.

These are two separate ways of interacting with the people and world around you. Neither is right or wrong, and the preferences are part of your DNA, just like your hair color. While you can become more outgoing or a great public speaker, if you're an introvert, you'll still recharge through alone time. Likewise, extroverts can enjoy being alone or doing things on their own, but they'll gain their energy through time spent in the world and connecting with people.

After reading the story a couple of times, ask your child how Toot and Puddle are different. Do they like the same things? Where does Puddle prefer to spend time? What about Toot? Ask your child if they would rather stay at home and do fun stuff like Puddle or travel the world and meet new friends like Toot?

Often, our society seems to promote extrovert tendencies like public speaking or being socially outgoing, and negatively portray introverts as being shy or reclusive. This perception is not a healthy way to view our personality differences and can be discouraging to introverts who feel different and less accepted or pushed to interact in ways outside their comfort zone.

Learning your way of recharging and your child's can help you create a routine that is healthy and fulfilling for each of you. If your child is an introvert, then daily story times at the library, followed by playdates and activities with others might set them up for a meltdown. Introverts are easily overwhelmed and exhausted by social events and settings and need that alone time to regain their energy.

On the flip side, if your child is an extrovert, staying home alone all day, every day might have them bouncing off the walls, talking nonstop, and needing to interact with others to feel fulfilled. Getting them out and involved in group activities might allow them to relax and enjoy their downtime more after recharging with others.

The same is true for you. Parenting is hard work, and everyone needs time to refill when they're drained. If you're an extrovert, be sure to schedule at least some of your child's playdates with other adults around for you to visit with. Plan social interactions to refuel yourself when needed.

If you're an introvert, finding alone time to recharge is critical. It's hard to do when you have small children, but it is much needed to keep you going. If you're an early riser, get up before your kids and savor that quiet alone time. If not, try to find moments throughout your day (when kids are napping or having their own quiet time) to unwind and just be. Or stay up a bit later and do something for yourself after they've gone to bed.

Reading a great story about two characters with different personalities and different things that bring them joy is a fabulous way to help your child learn that it's okay to be different. It's a good thing to know what makes you happy and to do it. Making positive comments like, "Isn't it great that both characters are happy and know what they like to do?" or "I love that Toot and Puddle encourage each other to do what they love" is a great way to give your child a realistic and encouraging perspective on introvert and extrovert personalities and how friendship can thrive even if friends like different things.

106

Geography: Travel - Climate

"Seeing" the world would take a long time! Toot has packed a lot of gear for his big trip. Ask your child what they would take with them on a journey around the world? Show your child a globe or world map. You might show them the land masses (continents) and the areas of water (oceans). You can show them where you live, and if you have family or friends far away, you can point those locations out as well.

Toot ends up in hot and cold climates as he travels. What would your child take if they were going somewhere hot? What if it was going to be quite cold? Write out a list of all the items your child would take with them and have them cross off or checkmark each item as if they were packing their bag and checking their list.

The classic "I Packed My Suitcase" alphabet memory game could be fun to play with your child. You start by saying, "I packed my suitcase with …" and fill in the blank with a word that begins with the next letter in the alphabet from A-Z.

Example:
The first person thinks of a word beginning with an A and says, "I packed my suitcase with an *apple*." The next player repeats the sentence and then adds something beginning with B. "I packed my suitcase with an apple and a bulldozer." The next player repeats and adds a word starting with C. "I packed my suitcase with an apple, a bulldozer, and a cat." Play continues until someone can't remember the sentence or list.

For younger players, you can say the next word without repeating the previous items in the suitcase. It's a great way to introduce the alphabet and alphabetizing (even though they won't realize it yet). It can be played anywhere, in the car, a waiting room, or a restaurant, making it a useful game to entertain children in quiet settings.

If your child is too young to play, you can say it to them. Be sure to make the items you pack so outrageous and silly that it is like a game just hearing your list. You can also use alliteration to make it fun by stacking two or three words that start with your next letter. For example, for a three-year-old listening, you might say, "I packed my suitcase with an angry alligator." Then, "I packed my suitcase with an angry alligator and a bouncing blue ball." Followed by, "I packed my suitcase with an angry alligator, a bouncing blue ball, and a colorful candy cake." You can still ask them if they remember an item as you play.

Teaching Tip:
As you read about the different countries that Toot visits, notice any particular interest your child might show about the various locations. They might get excited about Africa or Antarctica. Take their interest and natural curiosity and run with it. Find books from the library or pictures online to help them learn more about the world around them.

Language Arts: Correspondence - Postcards

Throughout the story, your child might notice the postcards that Toot writes to Puddle from all the various places he visits. They include a short message from the sender, a postmark, an address, and a stamp. We can't see the front of the postcards, but most postcards have a picture on the front of the country or state's scenery or a specific landmark associated with the area. Look at local gift shops, pharmacies, big-box stores, or airports for postcards that represent your city or local landmarks.

Ask your child how they would stay in touch with family or friends if they were traveling? We can call people on the phone, video chat with them, text them, or write them letters or postcards. Discuss with them how using a smartphone or computer allows us to talk to someone right away and not have to wait for a letter to go through the mail.

Writing a letter, though, can be a special way to tell someone that you're thinking of them. It takes a bit of time and effort to write out a message, stamp it, and mail it. Postcards allow you to send a quick hello without having to write out a long letter. They also usually give the recipient a glimpse into what you're seeing or doing (if traveling) based on the photo or image on the postcard.

If your child seems interested, you could buy a few postcards and let them color or "write" a message to family or friends and mail them.

Science: Hippopotamus

Toot meets new friends in Africa: a herd of hippopotamuses. The hippopotamus is a large, mostly herbivorous (eating primarily plants), semi-aquatic (spending large amounts of time in the water), mammal. Their name comes from a Greek word meaning "river horse." While they don't swim, they do have webbed skin between their four toes that allows them to move around the water more effectively and climb up and down slippery river banks. A hippo can take in enough air to stay underwater for up to 30 minutes! They spend their days in water and mud to keep cool and come out at night to graze on grasses. Share these interesting facts with your child or find a book about hippopotamuses at the library to look through and read together.

If you're playing the Animal Classification Game, create your own card by drawing or cutting out a picture and gluing it to an index card. Or use the hippopotamus card provided in the index to add to your collection.

Art: Movement and Motion

While Toot is meeting new friends in Africa, Puddle happily has his adventures at Pocket Pond. Ask your child, "What is Puddle doing?" while looking at the illustration of him ice skating. They may or may not recognize or know what ice skating is, but you might hear answers like, jumping, dancing, falling, flying. These answers show the artistic success of the illustrator in depicting motion and movement of the character.

Talk with your child about how they know that Puddle is jumping, dancing, flying, or falling. They may be able to explain to you that his feet are up in the air, or his arms are out to the side, or in front of him. If they don't notice or point out the lines around Puddle's arms, legs, and feet, you can show them how the lines are helping to create a sense of movement or direction. Even Puddle's whistling has lines going out from his mouth to the notes, showing the blowing air movement or motion.

Another thing in this illustration that helps us notice movement and motion is seeing six different moments of action on the same page. It's almost like watching a movie of a character skating across a frozen pond. If there was only one illustration of Puddle, it might be hard to tell if he is moving or standing still. It is the same as animation; if these six images were stacking and turned into a flip book and you flipped through the pages quickly, you'd see the movement like a movie.

For an older child, you can encourage them to draw something in motion by using lines or many moments and movements to show their object/person in action!

Science: Camel

On his continued travels, Toot is seen riding a camel in Egypt. Camels have long legs and necks and one or two humps on their back. These humps store fat

that the camel can use to survive when food or water is scarce. They live in arid (dry) climates that have a severe lack of water, enough to prevent or hinder growth.

If you're playing the Animal Classification Game, create your own card by drawing or cutting out a picture and gluing it to an index card. Or use the camel card provided in the index to add to your collection.

Geography: Oasis

In Egypt, Toot wishes Puddle could meet him at the oasis. An oasis is an isolated area of growth (trees and plants) in a desert, surrounding a water source (underground spring or lake). The available water and plant life provide a place that people and animals can live, or rest and refill water jugs on their travels through the desert.

Show your child a picture of an oasis. It's like looking at the opposite of an island. Instead of being a piece of land surrounded by water (like an island), an oasis is a small area of water and green growth, surrounded by desert land. If your child is interested, have them color a picture of an oasis, drawing water and trees, surrounded by dry tan desert.

Science: Maple Syrup

In Woodcock Pocket, Puddle is checking on his maple tree taps. Your child might find this picture strange. Why would Puddle be looking in a metal bucket nailed to a tree when the story is talking about maple syrup and pancakes? Your child may not know how we get maple syrup (other than from the store). Take this opportunity to discuss where pure maple syrup comes from and how it's made.

Several varieties of maple trees (sugar maple, red maple, and black maple being the most common) are used to make maple syrup. The trees store starch in their trunk that is converted into sugar, and rises in the sap in late winter or early spring. People drill holes into the trunk of the tree and place a tap (spout) into the hole. They attach a bucket to collect the sap. The sap is then heated over a fire to evaporate water from the fluid, which leaves the concentrated syrup.

If you live in an area where you can observe the syrup making process, that would be an excellent opportunity to help your child see that syrup comes from inside a tree and is harvested (tapped). Check with your state's conservation or natural resources department to see if this type of outing is available. If you can't see the process near you, or it is the wrong season, search online for a video (always remember to preview it) to share with your child.

Reinforce their learning experience through one of their five senses ... taste! Make pancakes, biscuits, or cornbread (or any other tasty thing) and enjoy a snack with your child that includes topping it with pure maple syrup!

Science:
Spring, Weather, and Seasons

Spring has arrived in Woodcock pocket and Puddle is having mud season! If your child knows about seasons already, you can ask why spring might be called mud season. If they don't have previous knowledge about seasons or don't have any ideas about why one might call it that, you can share with them the following information. (In addition, you can remind your child about what they learned in the Science: Dirt and Mud lesson from *Blue on Blue*.)

Two things happen in spring that create mud. The first is rain! Spring showers are frequent in most areas. Also, as spring arrives, any remaining winter snow melts. The added water from rain and snowmelt makes dirt turn to mud.

Here's a poem entitled "April" that describes spring rain. Found in *Voices of Verse, Book One* by Harry Flynn, Ray MacLean, and Chester Lund; illustrated by Marion Humphreys Matchitt.

Rain has such fun in April,
it patters through the trees
Talking to all the leaf buds
and robins that it sees
It splashes through the puddles
and skips along the walks
Goes coasting down the grass blades
and dandelion stalks
It dips in all the flowers
and when the clouds blow by
It paints with flower colors
a rainbow in the sky!

Science: Pigs and Mud

Why is Puddle so excited about mud season? Puddle is a pig. Pigs love mud. *Why* do pigs love mud? That's a great question!

Pigs have very few sweat glands and therefore don't sweat much. Ask your child, "When do you usually get sweaty?" They'll probably say, when it's hot outside, or when I'm running or playing. If they do, that's a great observation! We sweat when our bodies get warmer than they should be (98.6°F). The sweat creates water on our skin that evaporates and reduces our body temperature (makes us cooler).

Ask your child what they like to do outside in summer when it's really hot? They might answer with various water activities (play in the pool, sprinkler, splash pad, water table). You might ask, "Why do you like playing in the water when it's hot?" Yes, because it's cooling! You can tell them this is one of the reasons that pigs like mud so much; when they wallow or roll around in the mud, it coats their bodies and cools them down, just like jumping in a pool cools us off. Mud cools pigs longer than water or sweat would because the water in the mud evaporates more slowly than water alone.

Ask your child if pigs use sunscreen? Then giggle with them at the silliness of that question! They kind of do though, a natural version anyway. Getting covered in mud, for a pig, is like putting on sunscreen. The thick mud layer protects their pale skin from the sun and keeps them from burning. It also protects them from biting insects or flies. Lastly, researchers have found that wallowing in mud seems just to make pigs feel good and be a sign of a happy, healthy pig.

If you're playing the Animal Classification Game, create your own card by drawing or cutting out a picture and gluing it to an index card. Or use the pig card provided in the index to add to your collection.

Science: Penguins

Penguins are flightless aquatic birds. They spend about half their life on land and half in the water, feeding on sea life (fish, krill, etc.) that they catch while swimming or diving underwater. They live mostly in the Southern Hemisphere. There are many nonfiction and fiction books you can get from the library about penguins. If your child shows interest in penguins, take this opportunity to learn more about them together.

One fun, sweet, and informative penguin book to look for at your library is *If You Were a Penguin* by Wendell and Florence Minor. Another excellent book for learning more about penguins is *The Emperor's Egg* by Martin Jenkins.

If you're playing the Animal Classification Game, create your own card by drawing or cutting out a picture and gluing it to an index card. Or use the penguin card provided in the index to add to your collection.

Art: Masterpieces, Galleries, and Fine Art - Painting

While in France, Toot writes to Puddle, saying, "Art is everywhere!" The illustration shows Toot surrounded by statues and busts of pigs (because of course, it's a book about pigs) and in front of a painted portrait. The Mona Lisa (the painting seen behind him), is one of the most famous portraits in the history of art. Your child will not "learn" about it and remember facts at this point, but seeing the painting and having you point it out and mention the name, will begin to familiarize your child with a masterpiece that they will undoubtedly see again.

The Mona Lisa resides at the Louvre Museum, the world's largest and most visited art gallery. The Louvre is a historic monument in Paris, France. It was initially built as a castle and later converted to a palace for the French kings. Many additions formed the present palace seen today when visiting the Louvre.

In the 1980s, the museum's main entrance could no longer handle the volume of visitors. As a result, the architect I. M. Pei designed a spectacular glass and metal pyramid entrance with an underground lobby. It has become an iconic landmark of Paris, France. Just mentioning to your child that there is a museum in France called the Louvre (in the U.S. it's pronounced loov) is enough of an introduction at this age. You could also search online and show them a picture of the Louvre Museum, with its beautiful glass pyramid.

At home in Woodcock Pocket, Puddle is inspired by Toot's postcard to do a bit of fine art himself. He gets his easel, paint pallet, paintbrush, French beret (hat), a mirror, and a vase of sunflowers. His finished product is a colorful self-portrait. Ask your child what Puddle is doing? What tools does he need to paint? How did Puddle paint himself (since you can't see yourself)? Did your child notice the mirror behind Puddle? Looking in a mirror (or working from a photograph) allows an artist to paint his or her features accurately.

Now, provide your child with paints, paper, a paintbrush, and an opportunity for self-expression through art. They can try to paint what they see (a still life using flowers, fruit, leaves, etc.), or enjoy creating abstract art with no direction, or try their hand at a self-portrait! (As discussed above, a mirror is helpful for this.)

Social Studies:
Homecoming, Preparation, and Hosting

After many months of traveling, Toot wakes up and realizes he's ready to go home! When Puddle receives Toot's letter, the joy is visible on his face. His friend is coming back! The following illustrations show us something interesting: Puddle's preparations for the homecoming.

The definition of hospitality is the friendly and generous reception and entertainment of guests, visitors, or strangers. Either Puddle has a natural gift of hospitality, or his joy leads him to clean, cook, and decorate in expectation of his friend's return. He also readies himself with a bit of personal hygiene. Show your child the different ways that Puddle prepares his home (and himself) for a friend. What are the ways that your child could help you show guests hospitality? Maybe they could pick a flower or two from your yard to put in a vase or glass on the table. Perhaps they could help sweep or clean, to ready the house for guests. Or paint a picture to display or give to your visitor. Remember to teach and include your child in the **hosting process** when you have family and friends over to visit.

If Jesus Came to My House by Joan Gale Thomas is a lovely go-along book to read or reread as part of your hospitality discussion. This is a *Before Five in a Row* title. If you've already read it, you could remind your child about how the little boy imagines inviting Jesus in and showing him hospitality.

Geography: Countries Around the World

Toot went on a grand adventure and stopped in many different countries and continents around the world. For now, just seeing the landscapes and landmarks in the illustrations and hearing the names as you read is introduction enough. However, if your child shows particular interest in any of the places Toot visits, search for books from the library to allow them to adventure further into that country with you.

The countries and continents that Toot visits are listed below for your convenience. You could also point them out to your child on a globe or map to see how far Toot traveled!

- Africa (a continent)
- Egypt
- Solomon Islands (northeast of Australia, in the South Pacific)
- India
- Spain
- Italy
- Antarctica (a continent)
- Paris, France

Social Studies:
Celebrating our Differences and Friendships

Too often, we let our differences drive us apart. Toot and Puddle have found a beautiful way to strengthen and maintain their friendship—they choose to celebrate each other's differences!

"Here's to all your adventures around the world," said Puddle.
"Here's to all your adventures right at home," said Toot.

Ask your child if they would like to be encouraged by a friend to enjoy the things they enjoy instead of being asked to play/be/do something different. You can help them to begin encouraging their friends in the same way, to be themselves and feel accepted and appreciated, no matter what.

*Have your child place the **Toot & Puddle** story disk in Woodcock Pocket on the storybook map.*

TOY BOAT

Title:	Toy Boat
Author:	Randall de Sève
Illustrator:	Loren Long
Copyright:	2007

Summary

A little boy makes a toy boat. He does everything with his boat and loves it. One day the boat floats away into the lake. After a perilous journey, they are reunited and know that they belong together.

Bible

For Parent:

After reading the story, notice how each of the boats that the toy boat passes along the way go by without helping him—sometimes even spraying the toy boat with water or almost capsizing it with their wake. Until finally, the humble fishing boat notices the toy boat and has mercy on him by carefully helping to turn the boat until the wind can catch the sail and move the boat along again! Our story is a great reminder to be aware of those around us who might need help and to be the one to show mercy, even when others might pass by without helping. It has similar themes to the parable of the Good Samaritan which you can read below.

The Parable of the Good Samaritan

(This Bible passage is provided for the parent: it has graphic wording not intended to be read to your child.)

116

Luke 10:30-37, Jesus replied, "A man was going down from Jerusalem to Jericho, and he fell among robbers, who stripped him and beat him and departed, leaving him half dead. Now by chance a priest was going down that road, and when he saw him he passed by on the other side. So likewise a Levite, when he came to the place and saw him, passed by on the other side. But a Samaritan, as he journeyed, came to where he was, and when he saw him, he had compassion. He went to him and bound up his wounds, pouring on oil and wine. Then he set him on his own animal and brought him to an inn and took care of him. And the next day he took out two denarii and gave them to the innkeeper, saying, 'Take care of him, and whatever more you spend, I will repay you when I come back.' Which of these three, do you think, proved to be a neighbor to the man who fell among the robbers?" He said, "The one who showed him mercy." And Jesus said to him, "You go, and do likewise."

Of the three men that Jesus speaks of, the Samaritan should have been the least likely to help the hurt man. The priest and Levite would have known God's laws about loving your neighbor as yourself, yet they did not show love or compassion to the hurt man. The Samaritan would not necessarily have known or kept all the laws, and as someone who was discriminated against (based on his race/class), he could have done the same depending on the injured man's race or religion. But he did not consider his race or religion, only that he was in great need of assistance and care. He went above and beyond the minimum and not only stopped to help, but took the man to an inn and paid the innkeeper with his own money to take good care of the man and let him recover. Jesus teaches the difference between people who knew the laws and the ones who actually followed or lived them, as shown by their lifestyle and choices. Read the parable for yourself and be encouraged and inspired by the Samaritan's love for his neighbor and Jesus' challenge to "go, and do likewise."

For Child:

The toy boat ends up sailing through high wind and waves during the storm. That must have been a bit scary. The illustration of the little boat high on the waves brings another story to mind.

In the Bible, we read a story about when Jesus and his disciples get into a boat to cross a lake. Jesus falls asleep, and a storm comes out of nowhere. The wind and waves rock the boat, and the disciples are afraid. They wake Jesus up; then he tells the wind and waves to stop, and they obey him!

Mark 4:39, "And he awoke ... and said to the sea, 'Peace! Be still!' And the wind ceased [stopped], and there was a great calm."

It must have felt so comforting to have the waves stop and the water become still! It's so awesome that even the wind and waves obey Jesus. Do you think the toy boat would have felt better if suddenly the sea had been still?

As a memory verse for little ones, Mark 4:39 could be shortened to, "Peace! Be still! And the wind ceased."

Language Arts: Personification

After the storm, the toy boat is passed by many different types of boats on his journey. Each boat that passes him has eyes; for example, the tugboat has windows that "looked like tired eyes." The large boats also communicate with the toy boat; they warn, bellow, scream, or seem to say "Move along!"

Giving attributes of a personal nature or human characteristics to non-human things is called personification. The toy boat is the only boat in our book that doesn't have eyes or isn't personified in the illustrations. Why do you think that might be? Perhaps the illustrator didn't want children to be upset by the toy boat looking scared or sad.

Search-and-Find Game
Have your child play a search-and-find game on the second or third reading of *Toy Boat*. Search for eyes on each of the illustrations. What kind of eyes are they? Tired, fierce, pushy, etc.

Math: Counting Pairs

A pair of something equals two things. What comes in pairs? Mittens or gloves, shoes, socks, earphones. Have your child make a list with you of all the things that come in pairs. You can add to the list over days or weeks as your child sees or notices more things that fit into the pair category.

What body parts do we have in pairs? Hands, feet, knees, nostrils, ears, eyes. So if a pair of eyes is the same as two eyes, let's count how many pairs of eyes we can find in our story? (This concept is also discussed in the *Owl Babies*, Math: Counting lesson.)

Social Studies: Recycle and Reuse

What did the boy use to make the toy boat? Have your child listen as you read the first page of our story and then tell you what the boy used to make the boat. It was, "a can, a cork, a yellow pencil, and some white cloth."

The boy used items that would likely be thrown away and instead he put them together to make a toy boat. This is a smart way to find a different use for items that aren't being used anymore. See if your child can think of any reasons why we might want to recycle or reuse things? Examples could include saving money (making a toy instead of buying one), making less trash, or getting to create something. You can discuss how we can also recycle by putting cans, cardboard, and glass bottle into particular recycling cans for the city to pick up or by taking them to marked drop-

118

off points. These actions help reduce the amount of garbage going to the dump or landfills and allows for things to be repurposed into new objects.

Show your child the recycle logo. Next time you head out to do errands, ask your child to search for the recycle symbol.

Science: Things That Float

The little boy made a toy boat from "a can, a cork, a yellow pencil, and some white cloth." Go on a "treasure hunt" around your home with your child. Collect random items (hair pins, rubber bands, a cork, a penny, etc.). Fill a sink or large bowl with water and talk about each item and whether or not you think it will float and why. This discussion is a peek into making a prediction. Your child will start to learn by thinking about it beforehand, and then seeing the result, of which things will sink and which ones will float.

Relationships:
Time Together and Apart

At the beginning of the story, we hear that the boy loves the boat and that they are "never apart." After reading the story once or twice, you might ask your child if the boat liked being held by a string and never let go? They may point out that the boat wondered what it would be like to sail by itself. At the end of the story the boat is so happy to be back with the boy. The boy has also learned to let go of the string every so often to give the boat a bit of freedom ... but the boat always comes back!

Like the boy and his boat at the beginning of the story, a common parental tendency is to try to protect our children by holding tightly to their string. Allowing children age appropriate freedoms is how they grow and learn. It also gives the parent opportunities to help teach a child resiliency. Resiliency, the ability to recover readily from adversity, is one of the most important things we can help our children learn.

Talk with your child about times that you get to spend together, like bedtime stories and snuggles, eating dinner together, or riding in the car. Spending time together is always a wonderful feeling!

Ask your child what are some times that you spend apart? Perhaps it's during Sunday school, or when Daddy takes them to the park, or on days you have to work. Sometimes being apart is lots of fun, and sometimes it's hard to do. Spending time apart is good for you and your child. It gives you both time to do something different and helps your child learn that it's okay to be separated from you occasionally.

Remind your child when it's time for you to leave that you both have important things to do and when you're finished, you'll both be excited to be back together ... just like the boy and his toy boat!

Science: Lake - Waves

After floating away, the toy boat bobs on high waves. In a lake, waves are created by wind. Fill a shallow pan or large bowl with water (or let your child try this in a bath). Have your child blow hard from one side or straight down into the center of the bowl. Or you can blow (if they can't blow hard enough to create movement), and notice what happens. How does the water move? If the wind is blowing hard enough on a lake like it would during a big storm, the water moves and creates waves.

When you stop blowing, what happens? The movement or waves stop. The same thing happens when the storm passes; the waves and the water become still again. (See the Geography: Bodies of Water lesson from *All the World* for additional ways to discuss lakes and waves.)

Learning Through Play: Transportation Toys

The boy in our story has a toy boat. A toy boat is one type of transportation vehicle with which a child can play. Ask your child what other kinds of toys have to do with transportation, or moving people or things from one place to another? Some of the items on their list might include: cars, trains, bulldozers or dirt movers, tractors, buses, planes, helicopters, garbage or dump trucks, police cars, or fire engines. There are other toy vehicles as well. Have fun compiling a list and adding to it with your child! If you have access to a toy catalog, you could have your child cut out pictures of different toy vehicles. You could even go on a photo scavenger hunt at a toy store or big-box store, and let your child take photos of all the different vehicles they can find.

Teaching Tip:
Create an imaginary scene in which your child can enjoy their vehicles. Make roads using painter's tape on your carpet or flooring. Lakes or streams can be made from construction paper. Alternately, scarves or fabric can be used to create rivers, streams, or lakes. Use blocks to build bridges over the waterways or make moutnains.

Learning Through Play: Toy Boats

This story selection provides an opportunity to play together with toy boats. If you have plastic ones already, play with them at bath time. You can also work together to make a boat for your child out of recycled items you have around your house. Plastic containers or waxed paper milk cartons (pint, quart) with the top cut off would make a useful floating base. (Do not use a can, as edges can be sharp and could cut a small child.)

Language Arts: Sequencing - Early Literacy and Executive Function Skills

Whether you make a boat, buy a boat, or play with a plastic boat you already have, encourage your child to act out and sequence the story through their play. Sequencing is a foundational skill that becomes a building block for so many other executive function and literacy skills! Children must learn to sequence before they can sound out a word or learn to read. Children also need sequencing to be able to follow directions.

Sequencing builds executive function skills such as working memory and attention span. Putting the events of the story in order is something you can encourage your child to do with any story you read, through re-telling the story (back to you), or acting it out with toys, animals, or dolls.

If they are having a hard time remembering the correct order of events, you can ask leading questions like, what happens to the toy boat first? How does the boat sail when the wind and rain push it into deep water?

Language Arts: Sequencing - Singing

Another way to practice sequencing with young children is through songs. After hearing you sing or singing a song themselves many times, your child begins to know what to expect. You can play sequencing games through songs by leaving out a word or phrase and letting them fill in the blank.

"Row, Row, Row Your Boat" is a classic nursery rhyme song that is fun to sing, and make rowing motions to, with your child.

Row, row, row your boat
Gently down the stream,
Merrily merrily, merrily, merrily
Life is but a dream.

Social Studies: Types of Boats

If your child is interested in boats, this lesson can help them learn some of the differences between boats. Do they have an engine or use alternate power like the wind? What is their purpose or job? What are they made of?

A **tugboat** is a boat that moves other boats around by pushing or pulling them directly or with a rope. They are powerful and solidly built.

Ferry boats carry people and/or vehicles across water. In areas where ferries have many stops, they are often called water taxis. Most ferries today have engines. People with oars or poles often powered older ferries. They would row with the oars, or push off the bottom of the stream, river, or lake with the pole, to move the boat.

A **speedboat** is a boat with an engine that allows it to go very fast. Speedboats are used for recreation (fun) and also for boat racing.

Sailboats, like the toy boat in our story, are powered entirely by the wind. When the wind is caught in the sails, it causes the boat to move.

The **sloop** that our toy boat sails near is a specific type of sailboat. A sloop is a modern sailboat that features one mast and two sails.

The final boat that ends up helping the toy boat is, "a humble little fishing boat." **Fishing boats** are boats that are used to catch fish in a lake, sea, or river. Traditionally, fishing boats were made of wood (like the one we see in our story), but wood is not used as much anymore because of the higher cost to maintain it and its limited durability. Fiberglass is more typically used for fishing boats today.

122

A few fun go-along books about boats are:

- *Richard Scarry's Boats* by Richard Scarry

- *Busy Boats* by Tony Mitton, Ant Parker

- *The Boat Alphabet Book* by Jerry Pallotta

- *Boats on the Bay* by Jeanne Walker Harvey

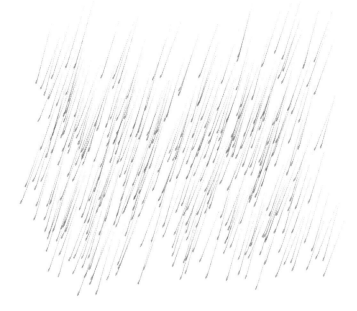

Weather: Clouds, Wind, Rain

Often when a storm is getting closer to us, the wind gets stronger and clouds begin to roll overhead. It gets darker as the clouds build. Notice with your child, the difference in the color of the sky and water between the illustrations at the beginning of our story. First, look together at the pages where the boy is holding his boat by a string, and then turn the page. Again, look at the sky and water colors when the boat floats away. And finally, the following pages where the boat floats high on the waves. Each time the pages turn, the sky and water get darker. Ask your child if they've ever noticed how it gets dark (cloudy) outside when it rains? That is because raindrops come out of the clouds. (For a similar discussion see the Science: Weather Changes lesson from *Blue on Blue*.)

Social Studies: Helping Others

The toy boat is alone and scared through the night. He's been pushed aside, splashed, or ignored by every vessel that he's passed. But in the morning, a humble fishing boat comes along with peeling paint and dents from being pushed around by other boats. The fishing boat knows how the toy boat feels and helps him, by turning the toy boat in circles until the sails catch the wind and it begins to move!

Ask your child which boat was kind and helped the toy boat? Talk with your child about ways they can help others. Some examples might include saying something kind to someone who looks sad, taking food to the firefighters or police near your home, or calling Grandma or Grandpa on the phone to tell them about your day and that you miss them. They could also be a friend to someone who doesn't have many friends, or clean up their toys after playing with them. When you notice your child helping others, mention to them that not only did they help or bring joy to someone else, but *they* also feel good inside about what they did!

*Have your child place the **Toy Boat** story disk on the storybook map on the Great Lake.*

124

Title: *Waiting is Not Easy!*

Author: Mo Willems

Illustrator: Mo Willems

Copyright: 2014

Summary

Piggie has a big surprise for Gerald. Will Gerald be able to wait for it? Will it be worth the wait in the end?

Bible

For Parent:

Isaiah 40:31, "But they who wait for the Lord shall renew their strength; they shall mount up with wings like eagles; they shall run and not be weary; they shall walk and not faint."

Waiting is not easy, and neither is parenting! The many needs of small children and nightly wakings take a toll on dads and moms. Running without being weary can sound like a miracle, even on the good days. Earlier in Isaiah 40, verses 28 and 29 say, "The Lord is the everlasting God, the Creator of the ends of the earth. He does not faint or grow weary; his understanding is unsearchable. He gives power to the faint, and to him who has no might he increases strength."

"But they who wait for the Lord shall renew their strength..." Isaiah 40:31. In this verse, to wait on the Lord means to trust in him; to put your confidence and hope in him in an expectant way; to know that he will provide strength when you are weary and power when you are

faint. What a merciful God we have that knows our weakness, or human limitations, and gives us power and strength from His endless supply when we put our trust in him!

For Child:
Psalm 19:1, "The heavens declare the glory of God; the skies proclaim the work of his hands."

For a young child, you could create a memory verse by shortening Psalm 19:1 to, "The heavens declare the glory of God."

God created a magnificent surprise for us when he created the heavens, the stars, the planets and galaxies! After reading the story several times, talk with your child about how Piggie is surprising Gerald by sharing God's creation with him. Sharing the splendor of the world that God has created, with those we love, is one of the most exciting things we can share! Ask your child how he can share God's creation with someone?

Take a nature walk together and observe the things God has made. Then see if any of them could make a special surprise or gift for a friend or family member. Help your child search for a unique rock to give to a friend. Or let them gather a small bouquet of wildflowers to surprise someone with!

Art: Line - Motion

The first page of the story has terrific examples of how an illustrator can use simple lines to show motion. Some of the lines are small or subtle, and your young child may not pick up on the movement depicted by them. For example, on the first page, Gerald has a circular ellipse line, by his ear, that is showing the motion of his head turning to look at Piggie.

Meanwhile, Piggie has thick looping dashed lines and little arching lines that are suggesting her actions, which in this case look like cartwheels! Ask your child what Piggie is doing. You could say, "Look, Gerald is sitting down. What's Piggie doing?" If your child says cartwheels, spinning, or walking on her hands, ask how they can tell.

Simple lines, showing motion, can be quickly and easily interpreted by all ages. During another reading of the story, after discussing this idea with your child, have them point out any lines they notice that show motion as you read the story. (If you've already read *Toot & Puddle* with your child, you can revisit the Art: Movement and Motion, lesson and look at how line and motion were shown in that story compared to *Waiting Is Not Easy!*)

Social Studies: Surprises

Young children love the idea of surprises. Often, like Gerald though, they find the waiting part almost unbearable! Discuss with your child whether or not they enjoy surprises. Which do they like more, surprising someone else or being surprised themselves? Why? Some children do not like the uncertainty that comes with being caught off-guard and prefer to be the one surprising others.

Usually, you have to be able to keep a secret to surprise someone. After reading the story, ask your child if Piggie keeps her surprise for Gerald a secret until it's ready? Would it still have been a surprise if she had told Gerald what it was? It wouldn't be the same, or nearly as exciting, if Piggie told Gerald early that she was going to show him the magnificent night sky.

Plan something together that your child can do, or give, to someone to surprise them!

Math: Guessing

Once Gerald realizes that Piggie is not going to tell him what the surprise is, he begins guessing. "Is it big? Is it pretty? Can we share it?" Guessing is a way of wondering or supposing something, without enough information to be sure of knowing the answer. It's the same idea as estimating something or making an approximation. Estimating is a high-level mental skill that your child will need for their future mathematics success. Isn't it amazing that it can be encouraged through guessing and built up from such a young age?

Guesses like Gerald's could lead him closer to the correct answer. Playing guessing games with your young child can be a great learning tool. It will push their vocabulary comfort zone as well since they will have to use targeted language to get closer to an answer.

Here are some examples of how a guessing game could help a young learner use specific vocabulary words:

Mom: Let's play an animal guessing game together. I'm thinking of an animal, can you guess what it is?
Child: A lion!
Mom: Good guess, but no, it's not a lion. Maybe I can give you some clues? The animal is green and likes to jump.
Child: A frog!
Mom: Yes, good guess, it is a frog. Now it's your turn.
Child: I'm thinking of an animal, it's brown.
Mom: What else can you tell me about the animal?
Child: It growls.
Mom: A bear?
Child: Yes, you guessed it!

You can see in the above example how randomly guessing animals without clues doesn't really get anyone closer to an answer. Using targeted language as clues is what allows someone to connect them mentally and then make an informed or educated guess. By taking turns giving clues and guessing, your child will develop their intuition, deduction, and vocabulary! This would make a great waiting room or car ride game to play together.

126

Social Studies: Waiting

After reading the story selection, ask your child why Gerald has to wait for the surprise? If they can't remember, read pages 16-17 in which Gerald says, "Wait? What? Why?" Piggie's response is, "The surprise is not here yet."

Ask your child if there's anything they're excited about but has to wait for? Answers might include the child's birthday, Christmas, or a special family outing that's coming up. You can ask if it's hard to wait for it to arrive. When it's something you're excited about, waiting is hard for everyone! Share a story of something you've had to wait for (or are waiting for). Hearing your story, and reading about Gerald's tough time while waiting, will help your child process that waiting is a normal part of life. These stories allow your child to develop intellectual empathy. Intellectual empathy is not acquired by experiencing something yourself, but instead, applied through hearing or reading someone else's story.

Social Studies: Big Emotions

Gerald has BIG emotions to being told that he has to wait. He cries loudly and says, "GROAN!" Look together with your child at the pages where Gerald groans. Discuss whether or not his tremendous emotional response affects anyone else? In each instance, his reaction is so big it hits Piggie and pushes her down. Talk with your child about how words can confuse or hurt others if we are not careful or kind with our words and responses.

What kind of emotions did Gerald have when he finds out he has to wait? Make a list together of the feelings that Gerald might have felt throughout the story when he has to wait. Frustrated, mad, angry, or sad might be on that list.

Ask your child how Gerald could have responded with a better attitude. If he had controlled his frustration or sadness, would Piggie have felt better about things too? Talk with your child about how we all have big emotions sometime—even adults! And even grownups don't always respond the way we should. An important part of being a good friend or family member is remembering to apologize when we say or do things that aren't nice.

Art: Night Sky Picture

Your child is likely accustomed to drawing or coloring on white paper. The story selection provides a perfect opportunity to create a night sky piece of artwork. You'll need black construction paper as your child's base. Use white crayons, chalk, paint, or pastels to mark on the black paper. Or you could use star stickers. Have your child draw/paint stars or place stickers across their black paper to create their own breathtaking night sky masterpiece!

You could use glow in the dark paint or stickers (without telling your child) and surprise them (they'll have to wait for it) when it gets dark with their glowing starry night picture.

Science: Day and Night

Gerald and Piggie wait all day for the surprise to arrive. After reading the book a time or two, look with your child at the pages where the white background begins going from gray to charcoal, to black. After reading the pages that talk about it getting dark and darker and not being able to see anything ... pause and ask your child what's happening. Ask them, do you know why it's getting dark? If you've already read the book through before this, they'll recall that it's getting dark because it's night time.

You can ask them if they've noticed how it gets dark outside each night. Ask them what they can see at night when it's dark. Yes, stars and the moon! You can remind your child that Gerald had to wait for the surprise because he wouldn't have been able to see the stars during the day.

Science: The Night Sky - Stars and Solar System

The night sky is spectacular! It's full of things to see … stars, planets, galaxies, and our moon. It's truly magnificent and provides such a fantastic experience for the viewer to feel their own scale in a different way. Looking at such a vast expanse, so far away from us, makes us feel small. We *are* small. Perhaps children have a better perspective on this because they are smaller than adults. Often we humans go about life as if the world revolves around us. When we pause and look up into the night sky, the heavens, we realize how little we are and how much creation is out there that we don't even know about or can't see! It's infinite.

If you live near a large city, the lights can make it harder to see the stars at night. Driving outside city limits, if possible, can improve the stargazing. Camping outside with your kids is a fun way to experience the night sky in a setting that is exciting and special.

For small children, you can explain that the planet we live on, Earth, is part of a "neighborhood" that we call the solar system. It includes other planets, too (Mercury, Venus, Mars, Jupiter, Saturn, Uranus, and Neptune).

The stars that we see in the night sky are part of the Milky Way galaxy, which contains our solar system. Sometimes stars form groups of stars that we call constellations. The Big Dipper is a constellation that is a simple pattern or form and could be pointed out (in the night sky) to a child, once they've seen a picture of it.

The sun is actually a giant star that is part of our solar system. The planets within our solar system rotate around the sun in a circular motion called an orbit.

128

The Big Dipper

Science: The Night Sky - Moon

The moon is made of rock and metal that appears brightly lit in our night sky because it reflects light from the sun. Without the sun's light, the moon would be dark. We can see half of the moon's sphere that is lit by the sun. The lighted portion of the moon that we see changes shape from a thin crescent, to half full, full, and then back again. These changes (called phases of the moon) happen each month (or 29.5 days, a lunar month). You don't need to teach this information to your child. You can mention it or not depending on their interest and age. Do remember, though, to point out the moon to your child during different phases and discuss the shapes that they can see.

- Crescent: similar to a smile or the white edge of a fingernail.

- Sphere: 3-dimensional, like a ball.

- Round or half: 2-dimensional, like a pizza, pie, or cookie (whole or half).

Have a snack of cheese or melon balls (spheres) and Oreo cookies (some whole and some cut in half, to represent the round and half-moon shapes). You could also make crescent rolls to go with a meal for a visual example of the crescent moon.

Additional Resources: Children's Books

If your child shows interest, you can look at more books or pictures together to continue their exploration of the moon, stars, and space! There are many astronauts, moon, and space-themed children's book available. Search your local library to find some that your child would enjoy. Here are a few recommendations to get you started:

- *Hello, World! Solar System* by Jill McDonald (board book)

- *Little Kids First Big Book of Space* by Catherine Hughes

- *Our Stars* by Anne Rockwell

- *There's No Place Like Space: All About Our Solar System* (Cat in the Hat's Learning Library) by Tish Rabe

- *Moonshot: The Flight of Apollo 11* by Brian Floca

Early Literacy: Moon- and Star-Themed Songs, Rhymes, and Poetry

Here are a few classic poems, rhymes, and songs about objects in the night sky:

Star Light, Star Bright
Star light, star bright, first star I see tonight.
I wish I may, I wish I might, have this wish I wish tonight. (Anonymous)

Below, you'll find the classic nursery rhyme turned lullaby song, "Twinkle, Twinkle, Little Star."

The lyrics of the song are based on a poem that Jane Taylor wrote around 1806, called, "The Star." Most children (and adults) are only familiar with the first or second verse of the classic song.

Twinkle, Twinkle, Little Star
Twinkle, twinkle, little star,
How I wonder what you are.
Up above the world so high,
Like a diamond in the sky.

When the blazing sun is gone,
When he nothing shines upon,
Then you show your little light,
Twinkle, twinkle, all the night.

Then the traveller in the dark,
Thanks you for your tiny spark,
He could not see which way to go,
If you did not twinkle so.

In the dark blue sky you keep,
And often through my curtains peep,
For you never shut your eye,
'Till the sun is in the sky.

As your bright and tiny spark,
Lights the traveller in the dark.
Though I know not what you are,
Twinkle, twinkle, little star.

Twinkle, twinkle, little star.
How I wonder what you are.
Up above the world so high,
Like a diamond in the sky.

Twinkle, twinkle, little star.
How I wonder what you are.
How I wonder what you are.

130

The poem below is a lovely reminder of many of the discussions you might have shared with your child while learning about the moon and stars. It references shapes that the moon can take: crescent, half, round, or sphere. It mentions the moon's friendly light (actually reflection from the sun) and that it can surprise you and hide (a new moon). Consider printing a sheet that shows the phases of the moon while you read this with your child.

The Moon Game

I'm the moon and I play a game.
I don't always look the same.

Sometimes I'm round,
A silver sphere.

Sometimes just half of me
Seems to be here.

Sometimes I'm a crescent,
Shaped like a smile.

Sometimes I surprise you
And hide for awhile.

Look up in the sky
For my friendly light.

What shape will I have
When you see me tonight?

– Author unknown

Science: Astronauts and Space Exploration

Ask your child if they enjoy exploring. What do they like to explore? Do they know that space is something that *can* be explored?! Would they want to go into space or to the moon to explore? Ask your child if they know who explores space. There are special people, called astronauts, that travel on spacecraft, up into the heavens to learn more about space. Then they share the information that they learn with scientists and with the general public to help everyone learn more about the wonders that surround them.

Pretend Play:
Journey to the Moon - Blast Off!

Pretend with your child that you're astronauts traveling to the moon. Stand in your spacecraft and begin a 10-to-1 countdown. Crouch down as you descend through the numbers and then blast off when you get to zero! Rising up high, on your tippy toes, into the sky! (This idea is also suggested in a lesson for *In A Blue Room*.)

Snacks: Star Cookie Cutter

With a star-shaped cookie cutter, you can create many starry treats for your child to enjoy. You can make cookies, of course, but you can also cut out cheese or lunchmeat stars. You can cut out full sandwich stars. Cucumbers, watermelon and bell peppers can also easily be cut with small star-shaped cutters.

An alternative or additional snack idea is to use pretzel sticks and arrange them in an outline of a star. Or draw a star onto paper and let your child put nuts, raisins or cheerios along the lines before enjoying their snack!

Language Arts: Literary Surprise

Waiting Is Not Easy! is written by Mo Willems. It is part of the Elephant & Piggie book series that he has authored. Another set of books Willems wrote is the Pigeon books. They include *Don't Let the Pigeon Drive the Bus* and *Don't Let the Pigeon Stay Up Late*, along with many others. Children *love* the Pigeon books because Mo Willems has brought the reader, or listener, into the action by speaking directly to them and asking them to interact and respond throughout the story.

In *Waiting Is Not Easy!*, Mo Willems has placed a special surprise for the reader (child) at the end of the story. On the very last page, after we've read the final words from Gerald and Piggie, the **Pigeon** appears, looking up at the sky and says, "Wow."

What a fun and exciting surprise! It's so neat that the author has placed a beloved literary character from another of his books in a place that the reader is not expecting it!

If your child is not familiar with the Pigeon books, you can always reverse this surprise. After reading *Waiting Is Not Easy!* several times, get one or more of Mo Willems' Pigeon books from the library and see if your child notices that it's the character that appeared at the end of *Waiting Is Not Easy!*

*Together, place the story disk for **Waiting is Not Easy!** on the storybook map in the stargazing area.*

Animal
Classification
Game

Use this game to begin teaching simple, enjoyable classification skills. After cutting out the images of various animals, attach them to index cards to begin classifying them into different categories. Group the birds together, the mammals together, etc. You don't have to teach the grouping name. This is an opportunity to discuss the similarities, such as, "Which of these cards show animals that have wings and a beak?" And then group those together. Or, "Which have fur, four legs, etc." From an early age, your child can have fun realizing that fish don't go in the "birds" card pile and that mammal-type animals are different from snakes. Remember that this is meant to be a very brief, enjoyable *introduction* to the world of classification, presented as a game rather than educational instruction.

Otter

Penguin

Bear

Deer

Fox

Pig

Beaver

Bee

Rabbit

Great Blue Heron

Camel

Hippopotamus

Duck

Turtle

Squirrel

Sheep

Owl

Firefly

Hedgehog

Stellar's jay

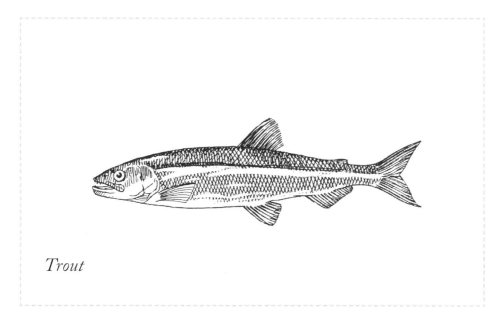

Trout

Copy this template to create your own animal classification cards.

Story Disks

More Before Five in a Row bridges a preschool-to-kindergarten gap by introducing your child to subjects and concepts that they will learn in *Five in a Row*. Geography, maps, and story disks are concepts and tools that your child can begin to understand and learn from without any added pressure of learning names of countrie or states. The Storybook Map in the back of your manual has locations that correspond to each of the *Mor Before* story selections. You can remove the map and the story disks and color them. You can also purchase color version of the Storybook Map and colored and laminated story disks from **www.fiveinarow.com**. The story disks represent each book and are placed on the Storybook Map throughout your time reading the story and enjoying the lessons that go along with it. For example, your child will place the *Bunny Cakes* story disk or the map at the Corner Grocer.

Ocean

GREAT LAKE

H.B. LAKE

W. C. POCKET

CORNER GROCER

More Before Five in a Row Storybook Map

Index

Recipes Index:

Teaching Tip Index:

Inspired learning through great books.

Five in a Row is a complete,* well-rounded, literature-based curriculum that takes your child from pre-K through middle school.

Current print products available from *Five in a Row* approved retailers:

For ages 2-4:
Before Five in a Row – Available from fiveinarow.com and Amazon.com

Before Five in a Row Story Disks (full-color, laminated)
– Available from fiveinarow.com

Before Five in a Row Storybook Map (full-color, laminated)
– Available from fiveinarow.com

For ages 3-5:
More Before Five in a Row – Available from fiveinarow.com and Amazon.com

More Before Five in a Row Story Disks (full-color, laminated)
– Available from fiveinarow.com

More Before Five in a Row Storybook Map (full-color, laminated)
– Available from fiveinarow.com

For ages 5-9:
Five in a Row: Volume 1
Five in a Row: Volume 2
Five in a Row: Volume 3
Five in a Row Starter Kit: Vols. 1, 2, 3 plus *Five in a Row Bible Supplement*

For ages 8 and up:
Five in a Row: Volume 4 (includes Bible Supplement and Cookbook)

Five in a Row **Supplements:**
Five in a Row Story Disks (full-color, laminated)
Five in a Row Bible Supplement (for Vols. 1, 2, 3)
Beyond Five in a Row Bible Supplement (for Vols. 1, 2, 3)
Five in a Row Cookbook (for Vols. 1, 2, 3 of both *FIAR* and *Beyond FIAR*)

For ages 8-12:
Beyond Five in a Row: Volume 1
Beyond Five in a Row: Volume 2
Beyond Five in a Row: Volume 3

For ages 12 and up:
Above & Beyond Five in a Row

Rainbowresource.com currently offers most *Five in a Row* print products as well as Literature Packages that go along with each of the *Five in a Row* and *Beyond Five in a Row* volumes.

Digital resources available from fiveinarow.com

Visit www.fiveinarow.com for additional digital resources and more information on the products above.

FIAR Notebook Builder
More than 120 pages of notebooking templates for all ages, appropriate for any topic or unit of study.

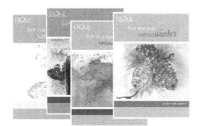

FIAR Nature Studies (Spring, Summer, Fall, Winter)
The *FIAR Nature Study* encourages your entire family to enjoy and explore the outdoors in all four seasons; it is a topic close to Jane's heart. Resources are provided to ensure that you can be a nature mentor to your child! It is a true unit study approach to nature studies; suggestions introduce you and your child to poetry, music, and art that tie in to the season.

FIAR Holiday: Through the Seasons
A treasury of traditions, ideas, and more for making your own special holiday memories.

Homeschool Encouragement Messages (Audio Files)

Inspiring messages from Steve on often-requested topics: Where Do I Begin, I Can't Teach All the Grades at Once, Making Your Children into World Changers, On Becoming Great Teachers, and High School and Beyond.

More digital products available at fiveinarow.com

You'll find other digital products at www.fiveinarow.com, as well, including a *FIAR Planner* and bonus units for Volume 4, as well as other *FIAR* products in digital format: *Above & Beyond FIAR*, the *FIAR Cookbook* and *Holiday* volumes, individual *FIAR Volume 4* units, and *Fold & Learns* for select *FIAR* and *Beyond FIAR* units.

You will need to add math and phonics/reading instruction to **Five in a Row.*

Visit fiveinarow.com for additional information on the latest products.

Made in the USA
Columbia, SC
27 October 2022